ESTATE PLANNING FOR THE RAPTURE

A PRACTICAL BOOK

by Tom Bousquet

Copyright © 2009 by Tom Bousquet

The Rapture, How Will You Prepare For It?
A Practical Book
by Tom Bousquet

Printed in the United States of America

ISBN 9781607917908

All rights reserved solely by the author. The author guarantees all contents are original and do not infringe upon the legal rights of any other person or work. No part of this book may be reproduced in any form without the permission of the author. The views expressed in this book are not necessarily those of the publisher.

Unless otherwise indicated, Bible quotations are taken from The Ryrie Study Bible, New American Standard Translation. Copyright © 1960 by Moody Press, Chicago, Ill. www.xulonpress.com

www.xulonpress.com

TABLE OF CONTENTS
(25,442 words)

Page no.

1. Introduction; what is "the Rapture of the Church?" Why a book about the Rapture?"..............9
2. How can you do Rapture Planning to get basic protection for your loved ones?..............17
3. Should you leave properties in your Will things to an address or entity rather than a person?..............21
4. Instructions to survivors, employees, employers..............25
5. What happens if you do nothing?..............31
6. How to prepare for your departure in the Rapture!..............35
7. How to prepare for the Rapture, and what happens if you are not taken in the Rapture!..............37
8. This book is not an attempt to convince you to believe in the Rapture: If it happens to you, you better be prepared. If it happens to others, you be prepared. If

	it does not happen in your life time, nothing is lost because you were prepared.	39
9.	How will I know when the Rapture occurs?	41
10.	The areas of impact and how to lessen the impact!	43
11.	Documents that you should consider preparation and execution.	45
12.	Estate Planning, Wills and Trusts, Executors, Trustees and beneficiaries	49
13.	Standard Powers of attorney (Form 3) and Health Care Powers of Attorney (form 5)	55
14.	Bank Accounts (checking and saving)	57
15.	Items on order and credit cards	59
16.	Notes, Liens and Leases upon which you are obligated (home, office, autos, boats, investments)	61
17	Stock retirement agreements and Business Buy Sell (or buyout) Agreements.	63
18.	401 (k), pension plans, Investment accounts (i.e. stock, bond, commodities, puts, calls, margin accounts, etc);	65
19.	Insurance Policies: (Life, annuities, fire, auto, home, etc.)	67
20.	Oil wells, real estate investments, apartments, office buildings, retail, warehouses, all of which need	

	management that controls the cash flow Land Titles, deeds, mortgages, title insurance companies.	69
21.	Pending law suits, bringing and defending them, and obligations that must be concluded	71
22.	Contracts	73
23.	Child Support, Alimony and Custody of Children	75
24.	Businesses owned: who is successor, salaries, notes payable, clients/customers, their records, operations and details.	79
25.	Pets, horses, cows, goats, dogs, cats, goldfish, birds, misc.	81
26.	Crops and plants.	83
27.	The effect of loss of medical personnel on the availability of quality health care.	85
28.	Trusts, Family limited partnerships, limited liability companies, corporations and nonprofit companies	87
29	At the Time of the Rapture, what if you or your loved or dependent ones are out of town, the county, the state or country; or in a hospital, a jail or an asylum and they are left behind?	91
30	Pregnancies, long term care, assisted living for persons left behind.	93

31. Loss of police and related services such as border patrol and customs agents, firemen, armed force personnel, congressmen, FBI, CIA, local legislators and leaders, national leaders, judges, appellate judges, supreme court justices. 95

32. Loss of strategic personnel such as air controllers, pilots, NASA employees including astronauts, ship, rail and airline personnel. 99

33. Normal Children (1-7 years old) (8-16 years old), (and over 16) Grandchildren, Spouses, Parents, Siblings, other relatives, friends, Handicapped children (1-7 years old) (8-16 years old), (and over 16) Grandchildren, siblings and parents. 101

34 Types of Instruction and Records to be left. (Instructions must be written to be effective) 103

35. FORMS 107

36. Bibliography 167

37. CV 169

Chapter One

What is "The Rapture of the Church"? Why a book about the Rapture?

In order to begin to understand "what is the Rapture", it will help you to read the following portions of a Christian Bible:

1 Thessalonians 4:16 "For the Lord Himself will descend from heaven with a shout, with the voice of the archangel, and with the trumpet of God; and the dead in Christ shall rise first.

17: Then we who are alive and remain shall be caught up together with them in the clouds to meet the Lord in the air, and thus we shall always be with the Lord.

18: Therefore comfort one another with these words."

And:

5:1 "Now as to the times and epochs, brethren, you have no need of anything to be written to you.
2: For you yourselves know full well that the day of the Lord will come just like a thief in the night.
3. While they are saying, "peace and safety!" then destruction will come upon them suddenly like birth pangs upon a woman with child; and they shall not escape."

Also: Matthew 24:21-44
        1 Corinthian 15:51-58

Even if you understand the words in the Bible, it will take more than a superficial faith in the words of the Bible to understand, much less believe, in the Rapture. A short hand rendition is that the Lord is coming back to earth at the start of the Tribulation Period.

Prior to or simultaneous with His arrival, born again Christians believe that the true Christians will be bodily taken to Heaven in the Rapture to live in Heaven until the Tribulation (while the devil controls the earth) is over and the Lord has his final battle with the devil and Satan and he and his follower are cast into the Lake of fire.

This starts Jesus' 1000 year reign before the final judgment and the rest of eternity. Some people might only believe a portion of this explanation or believe a different set of facts, i.e. that the Rapture will occur at the end of the Tribulation Period.

I am not trying to suggest the timing or the sequence. The exact timing and sequence are not material to my approach and my efforts to reduce problems for those who are not taken in the Rapture.

There are many books, pamphlets and sermons on what the Rapture is and what it will be. If you are not a born again Christian, the odds are that you don't believe the Rapture will occur, regardless of what you have heard about it. There is no requirement that you believe in the Rapture in order to read this book, and no requirement that you believe in the Rapture in order to follow some of the recommendations of this book and most importantly, there is no known requirement that you must believe in the Rapture before you will be taken up to Heaven at the time of the Rapture.

The answer to the question "do you have to believe in the Rapture before you utilize some of the recommendations contained herein?" is "No" because if you don't believe, and still take some actions on the recommendations, and the Rapture occurs, you can suffer fewer of the problems that can be easily avoided. If you take none of the recommendations and the Rapture does occur before you die, for example, if the Rapture happens in spite of your non belief, and suddenly your _____, _____, _____ (fill in the blanks) spouse, children, parent, key employee, your employer, your doctor, lawyer, banker, insurance agent, etc. disappear with many others in an event which can only be the Rapture, how can this affect your financial well being? (See chapters 10- 14)

Disclaimer:

No one can guarantee that the Rapture will occur just like they can't guarantee that it won't occur. No one living can accurately predict the year, month or day it will occur. This disclaimer is contained in the Bible (see Matthew 24:36-37,42). No one can guarantee that there is a Heaven and/or a Hell, but many millions of Christians have laid down their lives, and dedicated their lives to the proposition that there is a Heaven and that Jesus and the saints are awaiting them there. There is no requirement that you believe in Hell as Hollywood describes it; however, it would be hard to not believe that there will be a final judgment and some punishment for the wicked. I choose to believe the Bible that a lake of fire awaits Satan and his followers.

ALTERNATIVES:

If you don't believe the Rapture will happen, what are the alternatives?

A) If you die before the Rapture happens, and you did some Rapture planning, any preparations you accomplished will make life easier for your loved ones. The preparations will be good estate planning. The fact that the Rapture has not occurred will be immaterial, as all Rapture planning and preparations will be written to cover your death or your being taken in the Rapture.

B) If the Rapture occurs before you die, and you did no Rapture planning, you and the people you love, that trust you, and rely on you (emotionally, financially, or as partners, employees or employers, etc) are left with problems that may have been avoidable by a little Rapture planning.

> i.e. If you don't make some plans, you and/or your loved ones and dependent ones will have a harder period of adjustment for the reasons shown herein, because of the Rapture happening with no Rapture planning by you.

C) If the Rapture occurs before you die and you are Raptured, if you adopted some of the suggestions contained herein, then those you left behind should have an easier transition depending on what suggestions you adopt.

This book tries to show and explain how you can lessen the adverse impact that could occur. If you believe and want to lessen the impact of your Rapture on those left behind, this book will hopefully give you numerous things to consider in an effort to reduce the adverse impact when you are gone.

i.e. Whether you are a believer in the Rapture, or not a believer, if the Lord takes you in the Rapture, everything that you adopt that this book suggests, changes the effect of the Rapture, as it applies to your life, your business and your family and friends.

Anticipated Problems:

How are the ones left behind in the world going to react to the Rapture? I seriously doubt that they will be sympathetic to the persons Raptured and maybe less sympathetic to the family and property they left behind. The people who are left behind who knew you, might be sympathetic, but you can expect congress, the various state legislatures, judges and financial institutions (including life insurance companies) to adopt some laws that will make life a little harder for those left behind. I can imagine some spouses and children left behind will not have good feelings to the ones who were Raptured. This is just my educated guess, but how do you anticipate the people that Jesus did not take to heaven will react to those who were taken? I see anger and rage, envy, greed, jealousy, feelings of righteousness plus a realization of what they have heard may be waiting for them is real and horrible to imagine. The feelings that I do not anticipate that the average person remaining will have are: regret for their prior life, a desire to reform their way of life, compassion for the families left behind and any thought other than the greed and selfishness that has been their way of life.

Chapter 2.

How can you do Rapture planning to get basic protections for your loved ones?

There are so many various approaches to consider, it is hard to outline them all. Your age makes a big difference in your Rapture planning. This is also true of marital status, number and ages of your children and grandchildren, your parents, your financial shape, your business, occupation or job, your responsibilities, and your walk with the Lord. This also includes your spouse if you have one and whether you or they or both are probably going to be Raptured.

Your first decisions (and they are hard ones) is the analysis of who will probably be taken in the Rapture and who won't. Then the next step in your Rapture planning would be to draw your Will, Trusts and Powers of Attorney as discussed in Chapter 12 and 13 and contained in the Forms chapter at the rear of this book. Your decision should include whether you will utilize testamentary trusts and charitable gifts in your Will?

In the next set of decisions you will have to decide how to structure your bank accounts and investment accounts during your lifetime (chapter 14). Then just follow through the next chapters up to Chapter 33 and decide what you are willing to do now and then proceed to do what appeals to you, keeping other and further options in mind to implement as time progresses.

Your planning will not be perfect and will not be permanent. You should review your plan at least every six months for potential changes or improvements. The underlying idea is to make life easier for those who are left behind in the Rapture.

> I envision people getting together in groups, similar to a Bible study, to discuss the potential problems, the potential solutions and the decisions outlined herein. There should be interaction with insurance companies and with legislators regarding the potential problems, the potential solutions and the decisions outlined herein. You should also discuss your plans your thoughts, the potential problems etc. with your spouse, attorney, tax advisor, etc. You would discuss the

use of the various suggested documents and various forms subject to modifications under your state's laws. It would be impossible to imagine all the scenarios, the ways that your peculiar personal situation impacts the planning and the effect that your own state laws will impact the solution. If this motivates you to investigate and discuss the problems and potential solutions, you can find the correct plan for you. My e-mail address is published in chapter 37 and I would appreciate interaction and suggested modifications that could be utilized in subsequent editions.

NOTE: This book is not intended to cover planning to be implemented after the Rapture has occurred. However, if you are left behind when the Rapture occurs, you will still have time to do sensible estate planning to protect yourself and others who have been left behind. It is hard to imagine a world after the Rapture, if you are left behind. The book series "Left Behind" reflected how one man imagined this situation. How realistic his vision is, remains to be seen.

Chapter 3.

Should you leave property in your Last Will and Testament to an address or an entity rather than a person?

I realize that this may sounds little strange, but this chapter mainly applies to people who potentially will be leaving property to a charity or for the support of people who cannot earn a living. You must analyze the personnel in the charity if they are the main reason for you choosing that particular charity for your gift, or the custodian of the funds for handicapped or otherwise incapacitated persons.

When the Rapture comes, if you are taken and your Will is probated, if one of your designated charities was M.D. Anderson Hospital or the American Heart Assn., the particular personnel remaining should not necessarily make any difference in your choice; however if one of your charity beneficiaries is an evangelical church and 80% of its members and most of its staff will no longer be present following the Rapture, or if you designated a trustee who is taken in the Rapture, it could severely impact your intentions and plans. If you had named the pastor as beneficiary, he might be gone and the gift could lapse. The people who were left behind that will now manage the charity, church or trust could have very different ideas from yours. The same analysis should be made of other charities, churches or trusts you might want to benefit in your Will. Try to picture the entity after the Rapture and make sure what you imagine will suit your intents and purposes. You just need to think it through and discuss it with your trusted advisers.

It may prove embarrassing to analyze who may be taken in the Rapture and who may not. A conversation with a minister, trustee or a charity head which causes you to think that they may be left behind in the Rapture, probably should not be revealed to them. I cannot envision arguing over this subject, but it will require you to delve into their walk with the Lord. It may surprise you how others picture you in this regards. You may be assuming that you will be taken in the Rapture and others may assume you will be left behind. The world will be truly amazed at some of the Christians, including preachers, who will be left behind. It is going to require a good deal of prayers and searching the Bible for guidance to make your final decisions.

I suggest that when you make your judgment on who will be taken and who will be left behind, you still must include all persons you considered when doing your planning, regardless of whether you have the feeling they will be taken in the Rapture, or not. For example, if your brother Joe would be the first choice as your executor or trustee, put Joe first on your list. If he is left behind, he will serve you. If he is taken, your second or third choice will serve in his place, and you have covered both contingencies. What you would not and should not do, if you felt Joe was going to be left behind, is to name him (or her) to serve without listing any alternates. Then if you were in error on your judgment, your planning could be compromised. He could have found the Lord after you made your judgment on the probability of his being Raptured, or he could have died or become otherwise unavailable. That is why listing two or three alternates are always recommended, if there are suitable people available.

Chapter 4.

Instructions to survivors, employees and employers

You should be careful in preparing the written instructions you leave behind because if a probate court construes the instructions to be your Last Will and Testament, instead of the document that you intended to be your actual last Will, your Will can be compromised because the written instructions are usually much less comprehensive than the contents and directions in your Will.

Your written instructions should start off with a clause explaining your wishes if you are Raptured and disclaiming the instructions as your Last Will (see Form 4 at the end of this book). Then your instructions should continue with further instructions to your loved ones and your potential executor to describe your assets and their locations, together with the liabilities that may be facing your estate. You certainly should not give a copy of these instructions to anyone, except someone you know you can trust because of possible theft or fraud. For example, you can leave sealed written instructions which are not to be opened until your death or Rapture. Your instructions are basically an outline of your desires in the event of your untimely death or disappearance. Remember, if you are funding your succession with life insurance on your life, that the life insurance company might impact the situation by not recognizing your disappearance to be proof of your death. This can be discussed in your instructions and/or discussed immediately with the life insurance company to determine what their position will be and whether they have the flexibility that you desire.

For example, if you own or control a business your planning would include buy and sell agreements with relatives or key employees to protect the business from a disastrous shut down, due to your being taken in the Rapture, or to key employees being taken in the rapture, and/or relatives of someone taken in the Rapture fighting over control of the business.

This would include sensible provisions in your Will to implement the buy/sell agreement or to expand upon its provisions. Most business buy and sell agreements are funded by insurance. The life insurance policies are owned by the business itself. The insurance is on your life, if you are the moving force in the business and other key employee's lives. The life insurance will be used to fund the necessary price to buy out a key employee's stock interest from their estate on their death, or it can fund the costs of securing a replacement employee and cover any short fall in income due to the loss of the employee. The same is true with the policy on your life, it will allow the business to buy your interest from your estate on your death, hopefully leaving the business to continue with the key employees now in charge. This will keep you from having people with an interest in the business other than the key people that were important to keep with or without your death, and it gives your estate a way to sell closely held stock which is normally hard to do. In this case, it leaves the key employees in control of the business after your death, rather than they having to work for your relatives (possibly of uncertain business acumen). As I point out elsewhere in this book, there is a good possibility that a disappearance in the Rapture may not trigger the payment of the death benefits under a life insurance policy. Possibly a prior commitment can be obtained from the life insurance company and placed with the policy, but it might take new legislation or someone starting a Christian based life insurance company that will cover the Rapture, to solve this looming problem.

The main complaint by life insurance companies will be that with the occurrence of the Rapture there may be:

a) A widespread and a massive drain on the life insurance company's resources, and

b) [which is also a part of (a)] the disappearances will be persons from the ages of 18 to 100 with no regard for the insurance company's carefully drawn mortality tables that form the backbone of financial planning for the companies. For example they sell a $1 million policy to a person in his 20s for a modest premium which predicts that 90% of the people of the same age purchasing a policy will pay for a while and drop the policy, or that the person will live to the age of 75 and pay 50 years of premiums before there is a death claim. The life insurance companies invest these 50 years of premiums, and if their actuary was correct, when they pay out a million dollar death claim, they will have received $1,200,000 over the 50 years.

If many of these policies are paid out due the Rapture, far ahead of the predicted date of death of the insured, the insurance companies may face insolvency. The Insurance

Company of course will be sympathetic but will be unable to meet the huge, un-anticipated demand.

The analysis of the situation as a part of Rapture planning will be of great help to you whether or not the Rapture occurs before you die.

The content on the instructions that you leave depends on you and your spouse's special circumstances. (See chapter 29 for additional discussion on the matter of instructions).

Chapter 5.

What happens if you do nothing?

If you do nothing and die before the Rapture, there will be no effect on you from your doing nothing. This assumes that you will still do estate planning, powers of attorney, buy and sell agreements, family limited partnerships, etc. to properly protect you and your family; however, If the Rapture occurs during your lifetime and if you were not taken during the Rapture but have taken some recommended steps to lessen the impact, it may make some difference by lessening the impact of other persons disappearance that does affect you. Further, you should have spent the time necessary to choose a sensible and effective estate plan. Rapture planning is just like all other estate planning, it is only as good as the amount of quality, intelligent planning that you devote to the task.

If you are taken in the Rapture and have done no Rapture planning, it may or may not impact those whom you have left behind.

This can be possibly a spouse, children or other loved ones, someone who is dependent on you, your business, clients, your investments, etc. Only you can tell where it might be beneficial for you to act. If you study this book and find nothing that applies to you- so be it.. You at least tried! Much Rapture planning is merely Christian based estate planning. A thoughtful Will can accomplish much but can be handicapped by your executor or beneficiary leaving in the Rapture with you. The use of alternative appointments is an important safe guard.

I am aware that many professionals suggest a revocable living trust to solve your probate problems. In my opinion, living trusts have a purpose, but a limited purpose compared to other means of estate planning. This includes the use of the family limited partnerships, corporations and LLC's. A living trust is not a vehicle to cut estate taxes. This should all be discussed with a tax professional from the State of your residence before making a decision whether or not to utilize such a trust.

The only advantage to a living trust that I see, depends on which assets you place in the living trust. Placing them in a living trust means that those assets will not pass under your Will, but will pass under the terms set forth in the living trust. Normally the living trust becomes irrevocable on your death. If used properly, it can prevent people from attacking your Will on your death because there is little property left to pass under the Will, so why contest the Will. If the assets placed in the living trust are out of state real estate, it can prevent having to institute probate proceedings in the state where the property is located. Never put your homestead into a living trust (in Texas) because this usually takes away the homestead protection and the tax breaks on selling the homestead or at your death. The down side to a living trust is that normal handling of your assets while you are still living, after you have placed your assets in a living trust, can be cumbersome and expensive.

Chapter 6.

How to prepare for your departure in the Rapture!

If you have asked the Lord to come and live in your heart, if He is the Lord of your life, and if your life reflects your walk with the Lord, the chances that you will be taken in the Rapture are high.

Study the ideas in this book and see what applies to your particular situation. Sit down with your trusted advisors (which normally include your spouse, your attorney, investment adviser or C.P.A. or tax adviser). It would help if your advisors believe in the Rapture in order to advise you, but as long as you understand where they are coming from, it is not a necessity. To be effective for you, you just cannot utilize someone who ridicules your beliefs.

Normally your first step is to set out on a list the persons or charities that you intend to include in your Will. I say "Will" because this is the ultimate weapon in Rapture planning. Next you have to analyze each person and make a judgment as to whether they will be left behind or will they be taken (see Chapter3).

Next you have to analyze your properties and assets and the liabilities which you will probably have when you die or are taken in the Rapture (including insurance on your life). Obviously this will be a changing list as you buy and sell items, as values change, as liabilities increase and/or get paid off. This is why I suggest a periodic review. If you set a review each six months, the probabilities are that you will end up doing a review at 10 or 12 month intervals. It is still preferable to set goals and try to adhere to them.

Then you will have to decide how you will want to distribute your assets (and liabilities) among your family or other devisees (the first list). This analysis will include the use you wish to make of testamentary trusts and what use you have made previously of family limited partnerships, trusts, life insurance trusts, and beneficiary designations on profit sharing plans, IRAs, 401(k)s, etc.

You will also be appointing executors, trustees, persons to whom you are giving a statutory power of attorney (to use when you are still living), and persons to whom you are entrusting your health care decisions (Chapter 13)

Chapter 7.

How to prepare for the Rapture, and what happens if you are not taken in the Rapture!

The answer to this question will depend on what steps you have taken prior to the Rapture happening.

(A) Those people who are not interested in whether there will be a Rapture and do not believe it will happen, should be tolerant of those who do believe (i.e. spouse, children, friends, employees etc). Unfortunately people who interact with people whose belief system differs from theirs, many times are intolerant. I predict when the Rapture occurs there will be many people who deny that it happened- just like people deny that man has ever walked on the moon or that the holocaust has happened. But the things that those people do not believe should not bother those who do believe.

These people (who do not care or do not believe) should still be doing estate planning (Wills, power of attorneys, insurance beneficiaries, IRA beneficiaries, etc). The main difference will be if they designate someone who is taken in the rapture, they should have time to revamp their estate plan during the remainder of their life. It's the people who are taken in the Rapture that should have used some of the alternative planning I suggest in the book. Once they are taken they obviously cannot revise their estate plan. If big holes are left in their plan because of people being taken, then their plan will be thwarted or more difficult to implement

(B) The people who do not believe in the Rapture but still want to protect themselves and their loved ones from some of the effects that might occur, certainly will not prejudice themselves by taking some elemental precautions. If the Rapture happens before they die, they probably will not be taken in the Rapture but will be in a better place to understand what has occurred.

Chapter 8.

This book is not an attempt to convince you to believe in the Rapture: If it happens to you, you better be prepared. If it happens to others, you should be prepared. If it does not happen in your life time, nothing is lost because you were prepared.

There is an easy way to approach the Rapture. Just ignore it. Many people have died or will die without a Will or neglect to have their powers of attorney executed for the very same reason. They refuse to acknowledge that they will die before they are ready to die.

It is a given that if you live long enough you will start (in quiet prayer or loud earnest prayer) asking God to take you. That is if you still have the mental capacity to realize how bad your quality of life has become. This longing can be caused by loneliness for people who are gone or a crippling illness or problems resulting from an accident, or just uncontrolled depression. The people who suffer from advanced Alzheimer would be the ones to pray the hardest, but to our understanding, this is something they are not capable of doing, due to their condition. The same is true of people who are involved in accidents or who become incapacitated by disease, this is why everyone should have a health care power of attorney (Form 5). This must include a directive to a hospital and doctor regarding their not using extra ordinary efforts to save your life, if you will be a vegetable.

These are extremely helpful in the event of disability instead of death.

Remember to consider who might be Raptured and who on your list of persons appointed as your power of attorney might be Raptured.

Chapter 9.

How will I know when the Rapture occurs?

No one can predict when and how the Rapture will occur. No person knows when it will occur. So what are the ways that you will know that the Rapture has occurred.

A) If you are Raptured you will know as Heaven will be beginning of the most exquisite pleasure you can imagine.

B) If a country wide, state wide and worldwide disappearance of people occurs, if there is no other explanation, it will be the Rapture. If the people you know or hear about that disappeared, seem to be followers of Christ, it will help you in your understanding.

C) There are many natural disasters which will destroy much life, and even cause disappearances of a large number of people (i.e. the Tsunami in Thailand, the 1900 hurricane in Galveston; the two atomic explosions in 1945 in Japan) but these and similar disasters are obviously not the Rapture.

How are you going to act if the Rapture occurs and you remain behind? That depends on who you know who were Raptured and the amount of preparation that you did for the Rapture. Hopefully when the Rapture occurs, you do recognize that the end times are here and realize your future acts can be and should be pleasing to the Lord.

There is no question but that even after the Rapture, many of the remaining people will make Jesus the Lord of their life and will ultimately be transported to Heaven at their death or at the end of the Tribulation period when Jesus returns to earth for the start of his 1,000 year reign.

Chapter Ten

The Areas of Impact and how to lessen the Impact

How the Rapture will impact your life will depend on many variables. Of course, if you are taken in the Rapture, you will have graduated to Heaven; however, if you are not taken and someone who touches your life is taken, the manner in which you will be impacted will define the severity of the impact. If you are a husband and father and your spouse is taken in the Rapture, the effect could be extreme. If you or others did reasonable Rapture planning, under most scenarios, the transition can be smoother.

By using a power of attorney and Will suggested herein for both you and your spouse (or using other techniques) financial matters after the Rapture may be handled with far fewer complications (see Chapter eleven), which will make life easier for those you left behind.

The scenarios are countless but I predict that the persons who attempt a reasonable program of Rapture planning, and their loved ones that remain behind will find that the efforts have paid off.

As I mentioned elsewhere, if you die before the Rapture, your efforts will not be wasted, and if you are Raptured, your efforts will be a living memorial of your love for those that were taken and those who were left behind.

Chapter eleven

Documents that should be considered for preparation and execution

The most important documents to consider in doing Rapture Planning and/or any estate planning are:

1) Wills and Trusts (forms 1 and 2);

2) Powers of Attorney (form 3) including health care powers of attorney (form 5);

3) Banks Account cards including signature designations. These are obtained from your bank;

4) Instructions for those left behind (form 4) and Chapter 4;

5) Credit card applications. These are obtained from the various credit card companies.

6) Records preservation and retention, liability insurance continuing after death or disappearance, disposal of confidential records, etc.

7) Notes, Liens and Leases upon which you are obligated (home, office, autos, boats, and investments). These are usually prepared by the lender or the landlord;

8) Stock retirement agreements and Buy Sell agreements by owners of small businesses. These are normally prepared by attorneys;

9) Insurance Policy applications and ownership and beneficiary designations (life, annuities, fire, auto, home, etc.) including irrevocable life Insurance trust instruments;

10) Venture Agreements, entity charters and documents (i.e. by-laws, stock certificates, member certificates, minutes of meetings, various resolutions documenting actions and parties consents thereto) Notes and Security agreements when investing in oil wells, land investments, apartment houses, shopping centers, office buildings; the leases for execution by tenants, documents required by the Federal Government, State government, and City and County Governments, tax filings etc.

11) Law Suit petitions and answers, bringing and defending lawsuits;

12) Contracts, (Pending, needed, or required) including preparation, review and modification of documents, options and purchase and sale documents.

13 Divorce judgments and property settlement agreements, pre nuptial and post nuptial agreements, partitions of property between spouses, mediation and arbitration agreements regarding all manner of disputes including child support, and/or alimony (receivable and payable);

14) Documents governing businesses owned including provisions regards successors, salaries, notes, clients/customers, their records,

15) 401 (k), pension plans, Investment accounts (i.e. stock, bond, commodities, puts, calls, margin accounts, applications and signature cards with great care being given to 'payable on death' or other beneficiary designations);

As you consider this list, you must consider your spouse (and will they likely be Raptured?), your children, grandchildren, parents, siblings, relatives. You must consider your clients, customers and patients, your business associates, employees, and not the least, your pets.

Each professional and business person will have a different set of problems (Doctors, lawyers, accountants, realtors, bankers, business owners) as well as everyone else. Think of what you want to happen if you disappear unexpectedly and are not coming back! What will happen if your spouse, parents, partners, key employees, doctors etc. disappear unexpectedly and you do not? How will this affect you, your business, and your personal life?

Chapter Twelve

Estate Planning, Wills and Trusts, Executors, Trustees and Beneficiaries

Normally, when you die, if you have previously executed a Will, your attorney, spouse or executor will produce your Will and file it with the local court for probate. This leads to an orderly transition and spreading of your assets, income and debts among the people or institutions mentioned in the Will. If you are Rapture planning, you will have to examine the people you are assuming will be alive immediately before the Rapture, to see if they are likely to be Raptured. This is one of the hardest parts of this book, i.e. how can you judge whether someone will be Raptured? Will you be? This is also one of the most important discussions in the book, because it would not be wise to bequeath everything that you leave behind to someone who will probably be Raptured, or to an entity that will lose its main leaders to the Rapture, without making alternate provisions to cover the event that they disappear also. This is also covered elsewhere in this book. Also you should not name people to be guardians of children or of elderly parents or of handicapped persons, or appoint executors and trustees of your estate without naming alternatives. If the guardians, trustees or executors disappear in the Rapture, what will happen to those whose care has been entrusted to them. What will happen to your assets and obligations and/or your income stream in the event of the Rapture?

If it sounds like I am suggesting that you name dishonest persons or atheists as alternates (i.e. not likely to be Raptured), I am not. Once again this is a hard part of your Rapture planning. There is no way to know ahead of time if very young children (ages 1-7) will be taken in the Rapture. Logic suggests "yes", but it's a guess. What about older children? You have to analyze whether they will be taken up in the Rapture. You have to analyze charities, institutions and corporations to determine what effect the Rapture will have on their direction and intent following the Rapture!

For example, if you leave money or property to an evangelical church, will anybody be "running" the church after the Rapture? Will those who are left behind be people you want to handle your bequest? What about other charities? What about corporate executors and trustees? Will a bank be the same executor or trustee to which you are accustomed if certain officers are no longer there. You of course know that if you are Raptured (a) you can't take it with you, and (b) it might not make any difference to you _after_ you are Raptured as to what happens to people left behind or the disposition of your property that you owned at the time of the Rapture. Of course, no one knows if you will know what is happening to your survivors left behind on earth after your death or in the event of your Rapture. You only assume that even though you are in Heaven, you will have knowledge of and have compassion for their troubles and problems.

I realize that it truthfully will make a difference to you before the Rapture as to what arrangements you have made that are contingent on death or the Rapture occurring. It's normal to want the peace of mind which comes from thinking you have done your best to provide for those you will leave behind. There is peace of mind in having your affairs in order.

Who are the people who are listed as beneficiaries, trustees, guardians, executors and alternates in your spouse's and your Wills and Trusts. These individuals should be appointed to serve without judgment by you on their morals or lifestyle; however, you need some standard to use to judge as to whether a person is likely to be Raptured. It is hard to analyze intelligently and do what seems right, but remember, if you don't do Rapture planning your State law (or worse) will do it for you after you are gone.

Also, I need to point out that you should know that you can't execute a second or subsequent Will without voiding all prior Wills. You can have only one valid Will instrument but it can contain alternative provisions. (i.e. if the Rapture occurs before you die- Plan "A", otherwise Plan "B"). (See form 1 in chapter 35)

TRUSTS:

There are legally two main types of Trusts: (a) those that are established in a Will (testamentary) and therefore only become effective when and if the Will is probated and (b) those trust that become effective during your lifetime (inter vivos). The inter vivos trust is either irrevocable upon execution or else revocable before you die and irrevocable after you die. This should be written in the trust. Trusts are a fine tool to achieve certain goals (i.e. tax planning, long term protection of assets and beneficiaries, and achieving charitable purposes), but the downside of Trusts is that they often need to be either a testamentary trust (that is established in your Will) or be an irrevocable inter vivos Trust to achieve maximum tax benefits. A problem is that an irrevocable inter vivos Trust might cause unintended results or restrictions, unless proper Rapture planning is done. An additional problem is that it is normally a taxable event when any money or assets are contributed to a irrevocable inter vivos Trust before you die or when the assets or income are withdrawn there from,.

There are a number of alternatives to inter vivos trusts. One is a family limited partnership. Another would be one of the several charitable remainder trusts that offer alternatives that achieve tax savings though charitable donations.

I have prepared a rough draft of the terms that might be used in Rapture planning in preparing a Will (Form 1) which contains one or more testamentary trusts, and in preparing an Intervivos Trust (Form 2). These forms are very rough drafts and may not be proper or acceptable in your State or the one you are a resident of at the time of your death. You must show the filled out Form to your attorney or CPA, or both, that are assisting you with your estate planning, and utilize their advice. Do not rely on anything in this book for tax or legal advice. Use it as a discussion tool with your attorney or CPA.

Chapter Thirteen

Standard Powers of Attorney (form 3) and Health Care Powers of Attorney (form5)

Y ou have to realize that your Power of Attorney ("POA") becomes void on your death. How will those persons left behind (Judges, legislators, banks, stock brokerage companies, attorneys, etc) treat powers of attorney of people who disappear in the massive disappearance which is the Rapture? No one knows! If a person is Raptured and has left a power of attorney granting powers to someone who was not Raptured, if the Raptured person's body cannot be located, then is the power of attorney still valid? Or is the Raptured persons "death" presumed and the power of attorney void? If your power of attorney is void, then, will the probate court consider you dead and admit your Will to probate? What if the Power of attorney is declared void and the probate court will not probate your Will? I.e. you and others are gone with no proof or presumption of death! The Power of attorney can be drawn to try to cover this contingency, unless (which is not likely) it is unnecessary because congress or the states pass laws to anticipate the Rapture.

Wills, Trusts and Powers of Attorney should be written with options that apply (a) if the Rapture has happened and (b) if it has not happened. (Form 3).

Health Care Powers of Attorney can be impacted if the person designated to make decisions about your treatment level is Raptured, but you, the one executing the Power of attorney, is not. If you, the person executing the Health Care Powers of Attorney is left behind, and you are unable to execute another power of attorney, or delay re-executing a new Power of Attorney to replace the missing designee, you can lose the ability to execute a valid Health Care Power of Attorney (i.e. failing mental health, etc). This can be avoided if Rapture planning is done including naming a series of alternates individuals who are qualified to act.

Remember- just because someone is _not_ taken in the Rapture does not in any sense mean that they will not go to heaven when they die later.

Also remember, if they are taken, they will not be available to serve in a position of trust, as you requested.

Chapter Fourteen

Bank Accounts (checking and saving)

When the Rapture happens, if the principal wage earner in taken, then the arrangements that you made to cover the obvious problems that will arise will greatly affect those left behind. For example, if the main wage earner can no longer deposit a paycheck into the bank, or will no longer be there to pay the rent and insurance payments, how will the left behind spouse and/or children survive until matters are put back in order. Obviously, if proper contingent Rapture planning was done, the transition will be smoother.

Most accounts at financial institutions allow provisions for "the right of survivorship" or "pay on death" to joint signatories. Joint accounts are a common way to leave money available for those left behind, but sometimes this can be risky. For example, (the obvious problem) that your designated joint owner may withdraws funds from the account during your lifetime, without your knowledge or permission. This is unfortunately is not an un-common practice among relatives. There are many ways to try to protect against this contingency. A separate durable power of attorney can be a suitable method, but the power of attorney cancels on the grantor's death (but not necessarily on their disappearance). The problem of who to designate as a joint owner of the account (i.e. who to trust with this responsibility) is a difficult decision to make, and it must be done carefully to protect the availability of funds for the survivors.

Chapter Fifteen

Items on Order and Credit cards

We all hear the stories of identity theft. If you or someone close to you is Raptured, credit cards may be necessary for the immediate needs of a left behind spouse, parent or child. Notice must be given to credit card companies to prevent someone from stealing the identity while continuing the necessary credit access.

If you are the main wage earner, the credit card companies and other companies that offer credit will not be willing to factor in the possibility that you may disappear while owing them money. This means you must leave written instructions to your survivors (spouse, attorney or executor) who remain behind, setting out a plan to access your cash and other assets. You have to assume that if you are not present (i.e. have been Raptured), no one and especially financial institutions will extend you or your family additional credit. If you are not the main wage earner, you have the worry of the effect on you and others in the family if the main wage earner is Raptured, but you are not.

Because life insurance companies will probably delay payments on life insurance policies, this source of funds cannot be counted on. Your written instructions will probably need to be reviewed and revised at least once every six months due to changes that might occur. Depending on your situation, your plans should include access to contingency cash and credit. You must now evaluate what assets can be converted to cash, and what market value you assign to each.

The instructions should cover the contingency of the main wage earner or the main care giver to the family (or both) being Raptured. The instructions can include letters to those left behind (you will have to make some assumptions as to who will be left behind), including letters for your loved ones to take to your attorney, CPA, or banker explaining your desires and directions as to how they should act.

Chapter Sixteen

Notes, Liens and Leases upon which you are obligated (home, office, autos, boats, investments)

These are continuing obligations which must be paid in order for the ones left behind to survive, i.e. for investments including homesteads to be maintained and for business to continue in an orderly manner. This obligation ties into the handling of bank accounts, life insurance policies, investment accounts, trusts etc. by using some of our suggested clauses in Wills, power of attorneys and other documents set out in chapter 35.

In chapter fifteen, I suggested written instructions to those left behind with directions on where and how to access funds and which assets can be disposed of, and how to do it. I discuss this further in chapter 29. The need for written instructions should not be ignored and are especially important in the case of the Rapture (as opposed to death). The written instructions should be left by both the husband and wife or the father and the mother. Actually the leaving of written instructions is equally as important as a well thought out and executed Will and powers of attorney.

Chapter Seventeen

Stock retirement agreements and Buy Sell (or Buyout) agreements.

If there is more than one person that owns or controls the majority of a company's stock, stock retirement agreements and Buy Sell agreements are a common tool to protect against death, disability and un-welcomed offers to buy or sell all or part of the company. Once again, alternative planning can preserve the businesses, provide for orderly buy outs (by employees or relatives) and create income streams to survivors. Most plans are funded by life insurance. Obviously, if you disappear without prior Rapture Planning, those principals left behind (if they have bad motives) could take advantage of your loved ones following your Rapture. The remaining shareholders can move quickly to collapse the interest of your children or wife in various types of stock and assets for far less than a reasonable price.

Normally, most people who have equal (50-50) or close to it, divided ownership with others in a business will have a Buy and Sell Agreement. This is one way to assure spouses, workers, key employees, clients of the business lien holders and financial institutions that the business will not collapse and disappear on one person's death or disappearance. Normally the business is a huge percent of a person's net worth and the main source of income. That means in the proper situation, Buy and Sell agreements are as important as any other document, whether you are doing just plain estate planning or Rapture planning. With the realization that the Rapture is possible, modifying the Buy and Sell agreement document to cover the Rapture, only makes good sense.

Chapter Eighteen

401 (k), pension plans, Investment accounts (i.e. stock, bond, commodities, puts, calls, IRAs, margin accounts, etc)

This is where the majority of people's main non homestead assets lie. If you include your home and ready cash, this will include 95% of most people's estates. As I point out elsewhere in this book, you, before you start your planning, you must make an educated guess as to who will be taken in the Rapture. Discuss your Rapture planning with the people without explaining to them your reasoning as to the chances that they will or will not be left behind. Add their input and reasoning to your thinking. Then use alternative planning to structure your Will, bank accounts, 401(k), pension plans, IRAs, life insurance policies and investments accounts as I suggest elsewhere in this book, with more detail. Most 401(k), pension plans, IRAs, life insurance policies allow you, and most actually encourage you, to designate a primary beneficiary and also alternate beneficiaries, and this should be done. That is key to your Rapture planning. This requires the most time spent planning with the best input to solve your problems.

Chapter Nineteen

Insurance Policies (life, annuities, fire, auto, home, etc.)

Life insurance policies may or may not be quickly collectable on someone's life if they disappear in the Rapture. This is a gaping hole in your planning. Ask your life insurance agent what the various companies' present rules are. You can check with other agents to see if these companies handle this situation differently. Annuities should still be payable in accordance with its terms unless they are terminable upon your death. Fire, auto and home insurance will need to be maintained by survivors after the Rapture to prevent the cancellation of coverage. Possibly your being Raptured causes an auto accident (or other similar calamity). The survival of "heirs" able to collect on your insurance, or suits against the person who caused the accident inadvertently in the Rapture is something that needs to be part of your planning. Are Insurance companies and juries going to relieve a driver of responsibility if the driver disappeared in the Rapture while operating a vehicle? Will those remaining give them a fair trial? It is anyone's guess, but as is reflected elsewhere in this book, I am not optimistic that the persons who remain behind will be understanding or compassionate to those who were taken (and maybe their families who were not taken).

I am also not optimistic about Insurance companies voluntarily adopting a "Rapture friendly" policy. I have never discussed with anyone high up in major life insurance companies to see if and how they try to factor in a potential wave of claims from the Rapture. The companies factor in hurricanes and earthquakes, but these are minor blips compared to the tidal wave of claims following the Rapture. It does not make much sense to buy and maintain insurance which will be valueless when it is really needed. I am also not optimistic that legislators and congressmen who are asked to support legislation before the Rapture to address this problem will be willing to fight this battle. After the Rapture, the politicians who are left behind are not going to fight the insurance companies lobbyist to help the people (and their families) who have disappeared (and will no longer vote).

See Chapter 4 for my other thoughts on life insurance.

Chapter twenty

Oil wells, real estate investments, apartments, office buildings, retail, warehouses, all of which need management that controls the cash flow, land titles, deeds, mortgages, title insurance companies

The percentage of persons who own investments other than their house and an IRA is small, but important. If the owner of an apartment building, office building, etc. disappears, it can affect everyone who lives or works in the building, if the owner did no prior Rapture planning. If the ownership is in a company, then the problem can arise if the controlling shareholders disappear. If a building is being constructed, or the loan not in place for a building or signatures needed to close a loan or a purchase, a disappearance can be a financial catastrophe. The effects can be lessened by proper planning with the Rapture in mind. An example would be a buy\sell agreement and\or a last Will and Testament which provides for your unexplained disappearance and leaves directions as to who will do what and who will get or control what aspects of the investments.

The absolute uncertainty of the date of the Rapture will occur is the biggest obstacle to effective Rapture planning. That shows the beauty and simplicity of Rapture planning with alternatives. The Buy Sell Agreements can protect the "owners" but also offers stability to the spouse, employees and financial institutions in the event of death or disappearance. The problem of the Rapture happening in the midst of construction and or financing is not an easy problem to solve. An analysis of who may be taken and the effect on the project is the starting place. Utilizing an entity such as a corporation, LLC, or partnership should lessen the impact substantially by providing a platform that will survive your death or Rapture. Adequate professional help will be imperative to guarantee this is done correctly.

Chapter Twenty One

Pending Law Suits, bringing and defending them; and obligations that must be concluded.

If you are a party to a law suit, the disappearance of any of these persons, the plaintiff or defendant, or an indispensable witness, or the lawyer in charge of the trial or the judge of the court, can severely impact the outcome of the suit. Another problem could be if the jury has been empanelled and one or more jurors disappear. This shows some problems cannot be solved by Rapture planning while other problems can be solved or lessened, i.e. planning does not hurt. Thinking of various scenarios can help reduce the surprise and to some extent, the adverse effects of the Rapture on matters that are left behind.

If you have been damaged by some person's or entity's actions, all jurisdictions require that the suit be instituted within a certain period of time (two or four years normally) to prevent the running of the applicable statute of limitations of actions.

If a suit has been filed and service has not been obtained on one or more of the defendants, who have now disappeared, is a problem you can only hope does not happen. If you have an essential witness that will make or break your case, their disappearance (if their testimony has not been recorded on a deposition) can be catastrophic. If one certain lawyer is essential to the case, he can usually be replaced, but the timing can be extremely important. Also important is the amount of Rapture planning the lawyer has done to lessen the impact of his (or her) disappearance or death. Judges and jurors that are taken during the course of a trial can cause a mis-trial unless the remaining lawyers and available Judges will act quickly and honorably to solve the problems.

It is hard to describe the effects that such an incredibly wonderful event as the Rapture, as being catastrophic or devastating but this is certainly how the Rapture will appear to those who are left behind.

Chapter Twenty Two

Contracts

There are at least two parties to every contract. Some have multiple parties. Some contracts require people or entries to perform acts including paying money, acting in a certain way, furnishing services or goods, etc. The problems that would arise after Tribulation depend on the time and effort put in to prepare for the Rapture. It is hard to predict the problems that will arise because the party or parties who are Raptured will not be on hand to help in the resolution of problems. Some Rapture planning will accomplish making matters easier if alternative clauses are used.

The various scenarios are far too numerous to anticipate the problems that could arise. Wills, powers of attorney, but and sell agreements, corporations and partnerships are all forms of contracts and are treated elsewhere in this book. Clauses can be written into contracts covering the death of a party, so why not clauses to cover the disappearance caused by the Rapture. The clauses would depend on the type of enterprise covered by the contract, its intent and purpose, its makeup in number of participants and the financial contributions of each person thereto and most importantly, the effect of any of the participant's death or Rapture would have on the viability or ability to continue without them.

Chapter Twenty Three

Child Support, Alimony and Custody of Children

If this is applicable to your situation, what happens if the children (or some of them) are Raptured? What happens if one paying the support is Raptured (I hear many ex-spouses groaning- "no way-never them!!") or the primary managing conservator is Raptured. This can take some intricate planning that requires co-operation between all parties. It is obviously very important to have the funds continue to flow since life must continue for those left behind at the Rapture. It will be much more effective if both parents assist in the Rapture planning. The difficulty of ex-spouses agreeing is understandable unless they realize how deeply their and their children's lives can be impacted if they fail to do some Rapture planning. The hardest part will be deciding who it is likely to be Raptured, or will both be Raptured! What of their parents and the grandparents? Are they going to be amenable to your planning for the rapture and are they willing to be a part of your Rapture planning? I.e. if the ex husband is Raptured but not the children's mother. Are the ex-spouses willing to consider this? Has the provider of the child support provided for support payments from their estate or have they funded it with life insurance? How will the courts and insurance companies handle this problem in such situations? Will his or her estate be tied up for months or years, or will the Raptured person's estate support the children? How about alimony payments? What if the children (or some) are Raptured with the father, but not the mother? The mother would lose the income of child support and possibly alimony and not have the means to support herself. The possibilities are endless but all situations must be analyzed and serious Rapture planning accomplished.

The death of someone is sometimes unexpected (i.e. a car accident) but the percentage of deaths that are without some warning is small. Also the unexpected deaths can cause much heartache and grief because no one has had time to plan for it. This is one of the benefits of Rapture planning. People who plan for the Rapture did plan ahead. There are instructions on what actions to take, who to see, who to trust, where the sources of money are, etc. The ridiculous paradox is that a_ we know we will die someday, b) we know it is only good sense to plan for that day, but, c) thirty five percent of the people do nothing.

Chapter Twenty Four

Businesses owned: who is successor, salaries, notes payable, clients/customers, their records, operations and details

As you consider this class of problem areas, you must consider your spouse, your children, grandchildren, parents, siblings and other relatives (and will they likely be Raptured?) You must consider your clients, customers, bankers, friends, etc. It is very important to plan and document how all the myriad of contingencies will be handled in an event such as the death or Rapture of a principal, collapse of financing due to a parties Rapture, loss of peculiar talents or connections due to a person being Raptured. Much of the Rapture planning all people should have done by the time they die, will be helpful but of all the scenario's, the failure of life insurance companies paying insurance, inability to continue with powers of attorney, or inability to probate Wills are some problems that cannot be fully protected against. These problems, tied in with the effect of Rapture on the world economy can offset the most careful planning., Rapture planning requires serious planning with various professionals in order to do the most effective Rapture planning.

Successors in closely held businesses can be handled by buy and sell agreements but what if you own 100% of a business and have not groomed anyone to replace you? You would not have a buy and sell agreement but does your business just close on your death or Rapture? Who can step in and hire someone competent to keep the business afloat? What salaries are to be continued, increased or stopped by firing of employees.

Who will maintain the records of the business and its clients if the business closes? Can the business be sold? Are some records confidential or permanent (i.e. cannot be destroyed)? Are there instructions left behind covering how to salvage the investments and protect the ones left behind?

Chapter Twenty Five

Pets, horses, cows, goats, dogs, cats, goldfish, birds, misc.

Once you are Raptured you probably will not be concerned with the well being of things you left behind, least of all your pets. Now before I am burned in effigy, note I said probably. If you are in the presence of God and all the saints, plus your long dead relatives, and now know the answers to all the questions of the ages, where time means nothing to you, how will the problems of those left on earth seem in comparison?

I realize the average person will want some Rapture planning to protect their loved ones, including pets and animals, left behind. It sounds elemental- someone will always step up and take care of your pets, but the costs of caring for them and the sorting out or multiple claims or desires for certain pets and animal came be anticipated and directed.

We have all read of people who leave money to take care of a pet, but is this really what you are inclined to do? This solution should only be handled by written instructions to friends and family setting out a reasonable Plan (i.e. who gets what and what should be sold).

Chapter Twenty Six

Crops and plants

Farmers who might be Raptured can do Rapture planning and instructions that would cover protecting the investment in crops for the benefit for those left behind.

On the other hand are the people who have spent countless hours and big bucks on their plant collections (ranging from Orchids to Tomato plants) and other hobbies. Certainly, there are instructions which could help friends and relatives understand your wishes. For example, in your Will, plus separate instructions, you could discuss the potential crops and (a) designate who would harvest them, (b) replant or trim, re pot, mulch or otherwise protect or continue such plants or crops. (c) Designate how to handle the sale and proceeds, if applicable. The instructions would normally only be effective on your death or Rapture, and should take into consideration that may be taken with you.

This particular Chapter will not apply to very many people but is important to alert the few as to a rationale course of action.

Chapter Twenty Seven

The Effect of loss of medical personnel on the availability of quality health care

This concern covers physicians, surgeons, dentists, nurses, support technicians and other support staff, ambulance drivers and attendants, and all the people necessary to keep the medical care efficient and effective.

There is no way to estimate who or how many of these persons will be Raptured, nor what the impact will be upon you (assuming you were not taken). For example, you could be perfectly healthy at the time of Rapture, and thereafter have to seek major medical or dental care.

We have no idea how the health insurance companies and long term care providers will be impacted by the Rapture. As I discuss in other chapters, we have no idea at this time how Life insurance companies are going to react to the massive disappearance of insureds (and beneficiaries). These same companies that also pay health insurance claims, may find their capital impaired by this large loss. Will the Federal government (and tax payers) have any money for a "bailout"?

In the event of the Rapture, the health insurance companies will lose a great number of their insureds, but it will not trigger the claims for payment that would and could over whelm a life insurance company.

I anticipate the Rapture will cause a great shortage of competent medical personnel and practitioners. I of course may be wrong, but between socialized medicine and the Rapture, I think my concerns are justified.

Chapter Twenty Eight

Trusts, Family Limited Partnerships, limited liability companies and corporations and nonprofit corporations as owners of assets.

As previously discussed (chapter 12) trusts are effective to continue ownership of assets regardless of the death or disappearance of the person establishing the trust. The same is true where the beneficiary or some of them are not taken in the Rapture. The terms of the trust can: establish substitute trustees, beneficiaries, irrevocability, events which terminate the trust and the distribution of income during the life of the trust and distribution of assets on termination. An irrevocable trust has certain taxable consequences upon both the funding of the trust and on the termination and distribution of the corpus. These tax consequences must be discussed with your local tax advisor.

Family limited partnerships have more tax advantages than a trust (under the present interpretation of the Tax Code) and have certain advantages which can reduce potential estate tax liabilities. The family limited partnership continues (assuming the articles provide this) in spite of the death of a general partner or a limited partner. The general partner of a family limited partnership can be an LLC if desired (i.e. will not die) which will give the partnership a longer life.

The terms can establish substitute general partners, limited partners, events which can terminate the partnership and cover the distribution of income during the life of the partnership and plans for distribution of assets on termination. The partnership is revocable like some trusts. This feature of being revocable does not affect the partnership's tax consequences like it does those of a trust.

Limited liability companies (LLC) and regular corporations are the most common choice of those trying to select a type of entity that hold and operate assets, or businesses. The choice of which entity would best suit your proposes is not covered by this book. The reason for this is that each person's situation is subject to too many variables. The advantages gained by placing significant assets into an entity must be considered in Rapture Planning.

Nonprofit corporations can be used but the use must be thought out in advance. If you are interested in designating a charity (church, foundation etc.) as a large interest holder in the nonprofit corporation (either ownership or as recipient of distributions), then a nonprofit corporation is certainly worth considering. Trusts, LLC's and partnerships can also achieve successful charity ownership of assets or distributions. There are many trusts which are specifically structured for charitable giving that have excellent tax benefits, but that is far beyond the scope of this book. Specific tax advice would be necessary regarding these various entities. Of course, most large charities have representatives or departments that are prepared to discuss giving plans with people seeking to make gifts to them.

Many have self explanatory brochures but after you have reviewed them, you still need to get with your own tax advisor.

This chapter applies to persons who have been blessed with large estates and who wish to achieve some significant charitable giving. Smaller gifts that are to only be effective on your death or disappearance can usually be handled as a specific bequest in a Will.

Non profit corporations can own and operate assets such as a business. Normally a nonprofit corporation does not have share holders but the nonprofit corporation can have voting members and directors who retain and exercise control over the non profit's income and assets. It has been my experience that nonprofit corporations are for charitable ventures and not for running a normal for profit business. A nonprofit corporation is normally the only type of entity that can obtain an exemption from paying federal income taxes and state franchise taxes. Most importantly, if they get the exemption granted to the corporation (and only in that event) they are qualified to accept donations which are deductable on the donor's tax return.

Chapter Twenty Nine

At the time of the Rapture, what if you or your loved or dependent ones are out of town, the county, the state or country, or in a hospital, a jail or an asylum and they are left behind?

This gets us back to the problem of determining in your mind whether you will probably be taken and what the effect will be if you are taken or if others are taken (See chapters 3 and 16).

Assuming you have been taken:

a) In regards to your loved ones or dependent ones being out of town, state or country at the time of the Rapture, your written instructions to them would be desirable. They could also leave instructions covering the event of Rapture or sudden death, to their loved ones (including you) who are left behind. These should be instructions that are the subject of meetings you have had with the individuals. Some written instructions should not to be opened until your (or their) death or Rapture. The variety of instructions is endless but should include: location of important papers, keys etc, access to credit and money, names of people to assist them and who to trust and who not to trust, and explanation of assets, insurance, etc.

b) The same logic applies to people in the hospital, but the reason for hospitalization and the extent of insurance will govern these instructions.

c) The principals are true of people in jail or asylums. These situations, if you are their caretaker or their source of support, normally call for trusts, partnerships and/or testamentary trusts (In your Will) for those unfortunates who are left behind. Your own decisions will depend on your own financial liquidity and other variables to be covered in your instructions.

Chapter Thirty

Pregnancies, long term care and assisted living for those left behind

Once again assuming that you have been Raptured, but the person or persons needing care are not, you might have the following concerns:

a) If you are pregnant and are Raptured, think how wonderful it would be to have that child with you for eternity. No one knows whether Children ages 1-7 will be automatically Raptured with you (or all children below a certain age). Children ages 8-18 are the ones with more potential for being left behind. These children have probably had some exposure to the Love of Jesus Christ and either accepted it or rejected it. Also, they are more responsible for their actions in rejecting the Lord in their life.. I certainly am not judging any person or persons, grouped by age or other grouping, but you should think this out and pray about it if it impacts you.

b) If your wife is pregnant and is Raptured, it will be wonderful for them. If your husband is Raptured, leaving you and the expected child behind, your life should be much easier if your husband did Rapture planning and you are provided for to the best of both his and your abilities.

c) If you are not Raptured and your spouse is Raptured, you can only hope that your spouse has utilized some of the Rapture planning, or that your transition will be smooth.

d) Loved ones in Long term care or assisted living care (Alzheimer patients, who are not taken in the Rapture) will fall into three classes. Those that have sufficient insurance to take care of their needs (including Medicare and Medicaid); those that have sufficient funds (i.e. a trust) that will provide such care and; the third group are those who have no funds, insufficient funds and/or insurance to pay for such care, and are not eligible for Medicare or Medicaid. There is the fourth group that is healthy at the time of the Rapture and later requires long term care. Each person and their spouse need to analyze their own situation and make plans accordingly and in keeping with their situation.

Chapter Thirty One

Loss of police and related services such as border patrol and customs agents, firemen, armed force personnel, congressmen, FBI, CIA, local legislators and leaders, national leaders, judges, appellate judges, supreme court justices

The extent of Rapture planning that you can do depends on the extent of your conviction that the Rapture will occur in the reasonable near future.

(A) There is no real way for you (as a person not in this grouping of professions) to protect against the disappearance of police, sheriffs, constables, firemen, border agents, customs agents, FBI, CIA, etc. The effect will depend on the number of people in strategic positions that are persons who are Raptured and the quality and dedication of those left behind.

We can only be assured that the Devil and his minions will not be Raptured, so crime should be as bad (or worse) than ever.

(B) The same can be said for the Armed Forces (Army, Navy, Air Force, Marines and Coast Guard). The consequence which would happen in the event of Armed Forces reduction would depend on whether we were at war, the risk of war, the extent of terrorist and Islamic extremists, and the extent that the Armed Forces were crippled by disappearances. The Armed Forces may have contingent plans but this is doubtful on a large scale. Of course, the other countries of the world would incur some disappearances, but it would be hard to estimate the extent and impact, and foolish to estimate the extent and impact, with any idea of being close to correct.

(C) As to the legislative branch (City, counties, state and national) and national leaders - these people mostly consider themselves indispensable, so other than normal succession rules, I am relatively sure that no Rapture planning will be done in this area.

The one area where disappearance could be catastrophic (relatively) is judges, justices and lawyers who are in the middle of important, contested matters. The disappearance of key Judges, lawyers and witnesses or even jurors can cause well fought out cases that are unresolved, to have to be retried.

What Rapture planning can you do? Always have transcripts made of important meetings, trials, and court room proceedings etc. Make sure your lawyer has an "2nd chair" assistant in important litigation - so if the lead attorney disappears, the 2nd chair who remains is hopefully competent to complete the matter.

Chapter Thirty Two

Loss of strategic personnel such as air controllers, pilots, NASA employees including astronauts, ship, rail and airline personnel

This describes a very serious potential problem that can arise if there is a disappearance of a number of strategic people in the Rapture. There is no way to protect against a surgeon who is in the middle of an operation unless (which is not probable) hospitals start keeping some surgeons on standby as "spare tires".

The list of strategic persons who might disappear and whose disappearance would be catastrophic could be softened by some Rapture planning, but my guess is that business will consider this a necessary risk (i.e. the same as potential heart attacks, strokes, etc.). Hopefully most of the people who are Raptured will not be in positions that can cause great damages to others. I am not offering solutions and do not suggest that people modify their plans or necessary travel or surgery, but it is certainly something to consider as time moves on.

To carry this to extremes would prevent you from traveling by airplane and many other forms of transportation (i.e. what if the driver of a subway train or the driver of a car or an 18 wheeler are Raptured?).

Just make sure you have done your best to keep your business and affairs in order, that proper instructions are left to the ones who need them, that Rapture planning has been done and that the Lord is the Lord of your life and resides in your heart.

Chapter Thirty Three

Normal Children (1-7 years old) (8-16 years old), (and over 16) Grandchildren, Spouses, Parents, Siblings, other relatives, friends, Handicapped children (1-7 years old) (8-16 years old), (and over 16) Grandchildren, siblings and parents

There is no indication in the Bible of who will be Raptured other than the born again Christians. Many children are not born again Christians because it requires an affirmative act by the child asking the Lord to come into their heart and be the Lord of their life. The affirmation does not have to be public or disclosed to any person (pastor, parent or friend). No person can do this for someone else. No person can judge whether or not a child (or adult) has made a true affirmation, even if done publically, and whether the child has the requisite maturity to understand the act and/or whether the child was sincere. This is true of older children and adults also. I have no answer for handicapped children and adults that do not understand life, death, salvation or even that there is right and wrong. As I wrote earlier, you and I should never judge anyone's walk with the Lord. Their life should however reflect the walk with Lord and if it does not, it is between them and the Lord. If the handicapped are aware and can make judgments then it is between them and the Lord if they will be Raptured.

Only by thoughtful and careful Rapture planning will you be able to lessen the effect of you and/or other family members being taken in the Rapture.

Provisions in your spouse's and your Wills and powers of attorney should be made for children of all ages up to at least the age of 18, appointment of their guardians, provide for their support, education and living expenses. You can review chapter 12 and Form 1A for some ideas for Rapture planning. Such Rapture planning includes spouses, parents, grandchildren, siblings and special friends.

Just make sure you have done your best to keep your business and affairs in order, that proper instructions are left to the ones who need them, that Rapture planning has been done and that the Lord is the Lord of your life and resides in your heart.

Chapter Thirty Four

Types of instructions and Records to be left: (Instructions must be written to be effective)

A) Payments to be made (amounts, when and to who are paid)

b) How will funds become available to the survivors? (Direct payments and payments to others on behalf of a beneficiary, by an IRA etc.)

C) What happens to life insurance policies on your life if you are Raptured? How about policies on the life of your spouse and others who were Raptured- are the face value of policies paid by the life insurance companies when there is no cadaver upon which to make the claim of death. How long will it take the life insurance company to declare the presumption of death occurred, and the insurance company pays the death benefits? What about accidental death policies? Will these pay if the insured is Raptured (i.e. was the death or disappearance an accident?)?

D) The various matters that can interrupt payments of child support, payments on notes, alimony, allowances, and salaries are: a) the financial institution closes; b) the person who directs the payments is no longer there to properly direct the payments c); the funds are not there or, d) the person who is the intended recipient is no longer here (i.e. Raptured). The various scenarios include the person paying is gone, or the designated beneficiary is Raptured, but not the children.

E) What about medical care, medical procedures and impending births? Are the hospitals able to handle traffic with reduced staffs? Are medical and dental offices able to be adequately staffed?

F) What about the courts that have cases coming to trial? Are the judge's numbers reduced? Lawyers? Support staff? What about necessary witnesses and/or documents? You could write a hundred scenarios and still not cover all the problems which might occur.

G) What about the sale of securities? Are there instructions regarding disposing of securities and proper instructions regards the proceeds? Should the Investments be sold? Are the markets open? Stable? Are there sufficient brokers and investment bankers to handle this? Are they efficient and honest?

Are the brokers going to churn your funds in your absence?

H) Will your survivors follow your oral instructions? What about written instructions? What if they are not made in light of the possible Rapture? If the instructions are made in consideration of the Rapture, will survivors follow the instructions? Will there be resentment or revenge for being left behind in the Rapture?

For instructions to leave in the event of your being Raptured while your loved ones are out of the country, state or county are similar to the normal written instructions we are recommending and are covered in chapter 29.

Chapter thirty five

Forms

A) Wills

FORM 1A: "In the event I disappear with the reasonable assumption I will not return (for example, a large scale "Rapture" type disappearance has occurred), then I direct my then acting executor to review or create a list of my assets and liabilities (working with my accountant Gail Prather, CPA of Houston, Texas, if she is available, or her staff otherwise) and determine my surviving heirs and [then use a Trust for a period of time or direct immediate bequests to survivors] taking into consideration any persons with disabilities or of a an age where they will require assistance with their health, living and education needs. Any persons who disappeared at the same time frame as me will be considered to have predeceased me, and shall not inherit from me, but their surviving issue can inherit as hereinafter set forth in this Will. These provisions will prevail over the hereinafter set forth terms and conditions of the rest of this Will.

If some of my immediate family (as used herein to refer my spouse, children and grandchildren as applicable) are remaining behind including my spouse is left behind, I direct [such terms and conditions that you desire]. I.e. my property will pass to them as set forth in this Will including a pro rata share of any property left to someone who has disappeared in the Rapture.

If my spouse has disappeared in the Rapture, but my entire immediate family has not disappeared, those remaining shall inherit [in trust or outright as you specify] my estate on a pro rata and per stirpes basis if necessary to follow my wishes set forth hereinafter, my property will pass to them as set forth in this Will including a pro rata share of any property left to someone who has disappeared in the Rapture leaving no issue.

If all of my immediate family has disappeared in the Rapture occurrence, I leave my property and estate to [a) brothers and sisters, nieces and nephews, or (b) aunts, uncles and cousins, or (c) a list of individuals, and/or a church or charity (keeping in mind that will probably be left behind in charge of the church or charity).

Then follow with your normal Will and Testament provisions.

2) Intervivos Trusts (form2)

_____ & _____ REVOCABLE LIVING TRUST

THIS TRUST AGREEMENT is entered into on _____ _____, 2009, between _____ (the "Husband") and _____ (the "Wife"), of _____ County, Texas, as Grantors (the "Grantors"), and the _____ _____, _____, of _____ County, Texas, as initial Trustee (the "Trustee").

WITNESSETH:

The Grantors desire to create a trust to be held, administered and distributed in accordance with the provisions of this Trust Agreement. Accordingly, the Grantors have transferred to the Trustee, and the Trustee acknowledges receipt from the Grantors of the sum of one dollar in cash. This property, together with any other property which may hereafter be conveyed to the Trustee subject to the trust hereby created, shall be held, administered and distributed by the Trustee, upon the trust and for the purposes and uses herein set forth. The trust initially created by this Trust Agreement shall be known as the "_____&_____ REVOCABLE LIVING TRUST."

ARTICLE I - REVOCABLE TRUST

A. **Character of Property.** Property transferred to this trust which consists of the Grantors' community property shall retain its character as community property and shall be accounted for separately by the Trustee so that it can be returned to the Grantors as their community property if this instrument is completely or partially revoked. The powers of the Trustee over such community property shall be no more extensive than those possessed from time to time by either Grantor over such community property. Property transferred to this trust which consists of a Grantor's separate property shall retain its character as separate property and shall be accounted for separately by the Trustee so that it can be returned to such Grantor as his or her separate property if this instrument is completely or partially revoked.

B. **Distributions.** The Trustee shall hold, manage, sell, exchange, invest and reinvest the trust property, collect all income and, after deducting such expenses as are properly payable, shall accumulate and distribute the income and principal as herein provided.

The Trustee shall distribute the income and principal of the trust to the Grantors in such amounts as the Grantors may direct. All trust net income not otherwise appointed by the Grantors shall be accumulated and invested. If either Grantor becomes incapacitated, the Trustee shall distribute such amounts of the income and principal of the trust for the comfort, health, support, maintenance or other needs of the Grantors as the Trustee shall determine, in the Trustee's discretion, to be necessary or appropriate to maintain the Grantors in accordance with the Grantors' accustomed standard of living at the time of the execution of this Trust Agreement.

C. **Termination.** Following the death of the first Grantor to die, the Trustee shall distribute all of the separate property of the deceased Grantor and all of the deceased Grantor's interest in the Grantors' community property to the duly appointed executors, personal representatives, or administrators of such deceased Grantor's estate to be added to and administered as a part of such estate. Upon the death of the surviving Grantor, the Trustee shall distribute all of the remaining income and principal of the trust to the duly appointed executors, personal representatives, or administrators of such Grantor's estate to be added to and administered as a part of such estate, and the trust created by this Article shall thereupon terminate.

ARTICLE II - TRUSTEE APPOINTMENTS

A. **Successor Trustee.** If _____ fails to qualify, dies, resigns, becomes incapacitated, or otherwise ceases to serve as Trustee of a trust created under this Trust Agreement, and the Grantors fail to appoint a successor Trustee within 60 days as provided in Article II, Section C, then the _____ _____, _____, shall become Trustee of such trust.

B. **Removal of Trustee.** Prior to the death of the deceased Grantor, the Grantors (acting jointly) may at any time or from time to time remove the Trustee of the trust created under Article II, with or without cause, and may appoint a successor individual or corporate Trustee or a series of successor individual or corporate Trustees or Co-Trustees. After the death of the deceased Grantor, the surviving Grantor may at any time or from time to time remove the Trustee of the trust created under Article II, with or without cause, and may appoint a successor individual or corporate Trustee or a series of successor individual or corporate Trustees or Co-Trustees.

C. **Resignation of Trustee.** Any Trustee may resign by giving notice to the Grantors. While both of the Grantors are living, if the trusteeship of the trust should become vacant for any reason, the power to appoint a successor shall be exercisable by the Husband and Wife (acting jointly, or by the surviving Grantor acting alone) for a period of 60 days, and by the Grantors' children (acting by majority, or by the survivor acting alone) for an additional 30 days should both the Husband and the Wife fail timely to appoint a successor. After the death of a Grantor, if the trusteeship of the trust should become vacant for any reason, the power to appoint a successor shall be exercisable, in succession, by: the surviving Grantor for a period of 60 days; and by the Grantors' children (acting by majority, or by the survivor acting alone) for an additional 30 days should the surviving Grantor fail timely to appoint a successor. If no successor Trustee has been appointed within 90 days of such vacancy or such notice of resignation, then a successor Trustee shall be appointed by a court of competent jurisdiction.

D. **Expenses and Compensation.** Every Trustee shall be reimbursed for the reasonable costs and expenses incurred in connection with such Trustee's duties. Every Trustee, except one of the Grantors, shall be entitled to fair and reasonable compensation for services rendered by such Trustee in an amount not exceeding the customary and prevailing charges for services of a similar character at the time and place such services are performed.

E. **Waiver of Bond; Ancillary Trustees.** No Trustee acting hereunder shall be required to give bond or other security in any jurisdiction. If the trust created by this Trust Agreement contains property located in another state or a foreign jurisdiction, and the Trustee cannot or chooses not to serve under the laws thereof, the power to appoint an ancillary Trustee for such property (as well as any successor ancillary Trustee) shall be exercisable by the Grantors acting jointly, or the surviving Grantor acting alone, or by the Trustee if the Grantors are both not living or are both not competent to act. An ancillary Trustee appointed pursuant to this Section may be an individual or corporate Trustee.

F. **"Trustee" Defined.** Unless another meaning is clearly indicated or required by context or circumstances, the term "Trustee" shall mean and include the initial Trustee and any successor Trustee or Co-Trustees. Except as otherwise provided in this Trust Agreement, if two or more Trustees are named or serving hereunder and any one or more, but not all, decline or cease to serve for any reason, then the remaining Trustee or Co-Trustees, as the case may be, shall continue to serve in such capacity. In all matters relating to the trust created under this Trust Agreement, the decision of a majority of the Trustees then serving shall control. Any writing signed by the persons whose decision shall control shall be valid and effective for all purposes as if signed by all such Trustees.

G. **"Corporate Trustee" Defined.** The term "corporate Trustee" shall mean a bank having trust powers or a trust company having (alone or when combined with its parent organization and affiliate) capital and surplus in excess of $10,000,000 (U.S.), and the successor (by merger or consolidation) bank or trust company to any such corporate Trustee named herein or serving hereunder. If a bank or trust company is specifically named herein or was a corporate Trustee (as defined above) when it accepted its fiduciary position hereunder, it shall not cease to be considered a corporate Trustee because its capital and surplus presently is or later declines below the amount stated above. In any instance where a corporate Trustee is required to be appointed as a successor Trustee or Co-Trustee in connection with the removal of any Trustee or Co-Trustee, the instrument of removal shall contain the acceptance of the corporate Trustee so appointed evidenced on it. If a corporate Trustee is serving as a Co-Trustee, it shall have exclusive custody of the properties, books and records of the trust as to which it is serving, but shall make such properties, books and records available for inspection and copying by every other Trustee of such trust.

ARTICLE III - REVOCABILITY

While both of the Grantors are living, the Grantors acting jointly may by acknowledged instrument alter, amend, modify, revoke or terminate this instrument on thirty days' notice to the Trustee (unless waived). Furthermore, either Grantor's attorney-in-fact acting under a power of attorney may, while acting jointly with the other Grantor or such other Grantor's attorney-in-fact, alter, amend, modify, revoke or terminate any of the provisions of this Trust Agreement on behalf of such Grantor by notice to the Trustee. No gift is intended by either spouse in executing this instrument. All property transferred to the trust shall at all times (while held in trust or upon distribution from the trust or upon revocation of this instrument) retain its character as community property or separate property under the marital property laws of Texas; provided that the Trustee may presume that all property added to the trust by a Grantor while both Grantors are alive is community property unless stipulated to the contrary in the instrument by which such transfer is made. Upon the death of the first Grantor to die and after the distributions provided in Article I, Section C have been made, the surviving Grantor, or an attorney-in-fact acting under a power of attorney on behalf of the surviving Grantor, may by acknowledged instrument thereafter alter, amend, modify, revoke or terminate this instrument on thirty days' notice to the Trustee (unless waived). Notwithstanding any of the provisions in this instrument to the contrary, prior to the death of either Grantor, each Grantor, or an attorney-in-fact acting under a power of attorney on behalf of a Grantor, shall have the power at any time to withdraw all or any part of his or her separate property which is held in trust hereunder upon thirty days' notice to the other Grantor and the Trustee (unless waived) and no distribution of any separate property of a Grantor shall be made without the consent of such Grantor.

ARTICLE IV - TRUSTEE PROVISIONS

A. **Powers.** The Trustee shall have all of the powers conferred upon trustees by the Texas Trust Code, and by any future amendments to the Texas Trust Code or any corresponding statute, except for any instance in which the Texas Trust Code, as amended, or any such other statutory provisions may conflict with the express provisions of this Trust Agreement, in which case the express provisions of this Trust Agreement shall control. In addition to such powers, the Trustee is specifically authorized:

(1) To retain, in the discretion of the Trustee, any property transferred to the Trustee by the Grantors or any other person, including securities of any corporate Trustee, without regard to the duty to diversify investments under the Texas Trust Code and without liability for any depreciation or loss occasioned by such retention;

(2) To exchange, sell or lease (including leases for terms exceeding the duration of the trust created by this instrument) for cash, property or credit, or to partition, from time to time, publicly or privately, at such prices, on such terms, times and conditions and by instruments of such character and with such covenants as the Trustee may deem proper, all or any part of the assets of the trust, and no vendee or lessee of the Trustee shall be required to look to the application made by the Trustee of any funds paid to the Trustee;

(3) To borrow money from any source (including any Trustee) and to mortgage, pledge or in any other manner encumber all or any part of the assets of the trust as may be advisable in the judgment of the Trustee for the advantageous administration of the trust;

(4) To invest and reinvest the trust estate in any kind of property whatsoever, real or personal (including oil, gas and other mineral leases, royalties, overriding royalties and other interests), whether or not productive of income and without regard to the proportion that such property or property of a similar character held may bear to the entire trust estate; provided, however, that the Grantors may direct the Trustee as to the investments to be made by the Trustee, and the Trustee shall not be liable to any person for any losses resulting from following the written direction of the Grantors in investing the trust assets;

(5) To employ attorneys, accountants, investment managers, specialists and such other agents as the Trustee shall deem necessary or desirable; to have the authority to appoint an investment manager or managers to manage all or any part of the assets of the trust, and to delegate to said manager investment discretion and such appointment shall include

the power to acquire and dispose of such assets; and to charge the compensation of such attorneys, accountants, investment advisors, investment managers, specialists and other agents and any other expenses against such trust;

(6) To register and carry any securities or other property in the name of the Trustee or in the name of the nominee of any corporate Trustee (or to hold any such property unregistered) without increasing or decreasing the fiduciary liability of the Trustee; to exercise any option, right or privilege to purchase or to convert bonds, notes, stocks (including shares or fractional shares of stock of any corporate Trustee), securities or other property, and to borrow money for the purpose of exercising any such option, right or privilege; to vote any stock which may be held in the trust; and if two or more Trustees are serving hereunder and no such Trustee is a corporate Trustee, to open any type of account in such a manner that all activities associated with such account may be handled by one of the Co-Trustees acting alone;

(7) To enter into any transaction on behalf of the trust despite the fact that another party to any such transaction may be (i) a trust of which any Trustee under this instrument is

also a trustee; (ii) an estate of which any Trustee under this instrument is also an executor, personal representative, or administrator; (iii) a business or trust controlled by any Trustee under this instrument or of which any such Trustee, or any director, officer or employee of any such corporate Trustee, is also a director, officer or employee; or (iv) the Grantors or any Trustee under this instrument acting individually;

(8) To make, in the Trustee's discretion, any distribution required or permitted to be made to either of the Grantors, in any of the following ways when either of the Grantors is incapacitated: (i) to such Grantor directly; (ii) to the guardian of such Grantor's person or estate; (iii) by utilizing the same, directly and without the interposition of any guardian, for the health, support, or maintenance of such Grantor; or (iv) by reimbursing the person who is actually taking care of such Grantor (even though such person is not the legal guardian) for expenditures made by such person for the benefit of such Grantor; and the written receipts of the persons receiving such distributions shall be full and complete acquittances to the Trustee;

(9) To invest the trust assets in any life insurance policy or policies (including term insurance) on the life of the Grantors, or on the life of any person or persons in whom the Grantors have an insurable interest;

(10) To make divisions, partitions, or distributions in money or in kind, or partly in each, whenever required or permitted to divide, partition, or distribute all or any part of the trust; and, in making any such division or distributions, the judgment of the Trustee in the selection and valuation of the assets to be so divided, partitioned, or distributed shall be binding and conclusive;

(11) To release, in the discretion of the Trustee, any fiduciary power at any time, in whole or in part, temporarily or permanently, whenever the Trustee may deem it advisable, by an instrument in writing executed and acknowledged by the Trustee;

(12) To invest and reinvest all or part of the assets of the trust in any common trust fund of any corporate Trustee;

(13) To continue any business (whether a proprietorship, corporation, partnership, limited partnership or other business entity) which may be transferred to the trust estate for such time as the Trustee may deem it to be in the best interest

of the trust; to employ in the conduct of any such business such capital out of the trust as the Trustee may deem proper; to borrow money for use in any such business alone or with other persons financially interested in such business, and to secure such loan or loans by a mortgage, pledge or any other manner of encumbrance of, not only the trust's interest in such business, but also such portion of the trust outside of such business as the Trustee may deem proper; to organize, either alone or jointly with others, new corporations, partnerships, limited partnerships or other business entities; and generally to exercise with respect to the continuance, management, sale or liquidation of any business which may be transferred to the trust estate, or of any new business or business interest, all the powers which may be necessary for its successful operation;

(14) To execute lease, pooling or unitization agreements (including agreements of such nature extending beyond the terms of the trust) with respect to any mineral or royalty interest held or acquired by the trust; to drill or contract for the drilling of wells for oil, gas or other minerals; to make dry hole or bottom hole contributions; to enter into any operating agreements with reference to any mineral leases

or properties held or acquired by the trust; and generally, with reference to oil, gas and other mineral properties and operations, to enter into such agreements and to do all such other things (whether or not presently recognized as common or proper practice by those engaged in the business of prospecting for, developing, producing, processing, transporting or marketing oil, gas or other minerals) as the Trustee may deem to be advantageous;

(15) To transfer such sums of the property of a Grantor to an individual serving as agent or attorney-in-fact under a valid power of attorney signed by such Grantor (or to several individuals serving jointly as agents or attorneys-in-fact under a valid power of attorney signed by such Grantor) as such agent or agents may request in order to make gifts, which are specifically authorized by such power of attorney, on behalf of such Grantor;

(16) To select and employ, at the discretion of the Trustee but at the expense of the trust, any person, firm or corporation, engaged in rendering investment advisory services or investment management services, to furnish professional assistance or management in connection with making investments, managing securities, or making any other

decisions with respect to the purchase, retention, sale or other disposition of property or securities belonging to the trust;

(17) To employ a bank or trust company located anywhere within the United States, at the discretion of the Trustee but at the expense of the trust, as custodian or agent; to have stock and securities registered in the name of such agent or custodian or a nominee thereof without designation of fiduciary capacity; and to appoint such bank or trust company to perform such other ministerial functions as the Trustee may direct. While such stock or securities are in the custody of any such bank or trust company, the Trustee shall be under no obligation to inspect or verify such stock or securities nor shall the Trustee be responsible for any loss by such bank or trust company; and

(18) Whenever in this Trust Agreement an action is authorized in the discretion of the Trustee, the term "discretion" shall mean the absolute and uncontrolled discretion of the Trustee.

B. **Inspection.** All properties, books of account and records of the trust shall be made available for inspection at all times during normal business hours by the Grantors, or by any person or persons designated by the Grantors. The Trustee shall furnish written statements (which shall be deemed correct and binding one year after receipt) at least annually showing the itemized receipts and disbursements of income and principal of the trust, and otherwise reflecting its condition, to the Grantors.

C. **Notice.** Any notice required or permitted to be given by or to a Trustee acting under this Trust Agreement must be given by acknowledged instrument actually delivered to the person or Trustee to whom it is required or permitted to be given. If such notice concerns a trusteeship, it shall state its effective date and shall be given at least 30 days prior to such effective date, unless such period of notice is waived.

D. **Acts of Prior Trustees.** Each Trustee shall be relieved of any duty to examine the acts of any prior Trustee and no court accounting shall be required. Each successor Trustee shall be responsible only for those properties which are actually delivered to such Trustee. Each successor Trustee, upon executing an acknowledged acceptance of the trusteeship and upon receipt of those properties actually delivered to such successor Trustee, shall be vested with all of the estates, titles, rights, powers, duties, immunities and discretions granted to the prior Trustee.

E. **Reliance on Legal Opinion.** In acting or declining to act, each Trustee may rely upon the written opinion of a competent attorney, any facts stated in any instrument in writing and believed true, or any other evidence deemed sufficient. Each Trustee shall be saved harmless from any liability for any action taken, or for the failure to take any action, if done in good faith and without gross negligence.

ARTICLE V - MISCELLANEOUS PROVISIONS

A. **Additions To Trust.** The Grantors, or any other person, may at any time, grant, transfer or convey, either by inter vivos transfer or by Will, to the Trustee such additional property as he or she desires to become a part of the trust hereby created and, subject to acceptance by the Trustee, such additional property shall thereafter be held, administered and distributed by the Trustee in accordance with the provisions of this Trust Agreement.

B. **Incapacitated.** A Grantor or a fiduciary shall be deemed "incapacitated" if and for as long as (i) a court of competent jurisdiction has made a finding to that effect, (ii) a guardian or conservator of such Grantor's or such fiduciary's estate or person has been appointed by a court of competent jurisdiction and is serving as such, or (iii) two physicians (licensed to practice medicine in the state where the Grantor or fiduciary is domiciled at the time of the certification, and one of whom shall be board certified in the specialty most closely associated with the cause of the Grantor's or fiduciary's incapacity) certify that due to a physical or mental condition such Grantor or fiduciary lacks the ability to manage his or her own personal and financial affairs. An incapacitated Grantor or fiduciary shall be deemed to have regained capacity if there is a finding to that effect by a court of competent jurisdiction or if two physicians (with the same qualifications described above) certify that such Grantor or fiduciary is capable of managing his or her personal and financial affairs.

C. **<u>Right To Use Principal Residence.</u>** The Grantors shall have the right to use and occupy residential property owned by the trust created under Article II as the Grantors' principal residence rent free and without charge until the death of the last to die of both Grantors or until this Trust Agreement is revoked or terminated, whichever occurs first. Further, any such property (or any interest therein) shall be acquired by an instrument of title that describes the property with sufficient certainty to identify it and the interest acquired, and the instrument shall be recorded in the real property records of the county in which the property is located. This section shall be construed in accordance with the Grantors' intentions to qualify such property as the Grantors' residential homestead for ad valorem tax purposes by causing the trust which owns such property to be a "qualifying trust" as defined and described in Section 11.13(j) of the Texas Tax Code. This intention shall be overriding and shall control if it conflicts with the literal language of this section.

D. **Children.** The Grantors have one son from their present marriage, _____. The Husband has one son from a prior marriage, _____. The Wife has one son from a prior marriage, _____. It is the Husband's intention to treat the Wife's son as his son for all purposes of this Trust Agreement. In addition, it is the Husband's intention to treat the descendants of the Wife's son as his descendants for all purposes of this Trust Agreement. It is the Wife's intention to treat the Husband's son as her son for all purposes of this Trust Agreement. In addition, it is the Wife's intention to treat the descendants of the Husband's son as her descendants for all purposes of this Trust Agreement. Accordingly, all references in this Trust Agreement to the "Grantors' children" are to _____ _____, _____, _____ _____ and to all children hereafter born to or adopted by the Grantors. In addition, all references in this Trust Agreement to the "Grantors' descendants" are to the Grantors' children (as defined above) and to all of their respective descendants.

E. **Governing Law.** The construction, validity and administration of the trust created under this Trust Agreement shall be controlled by the laws of the State of Texas unless the Trustee designates the laws of another jurisdiction as the controlling law with respect to the administration of such trust, in which event the laws of such designated jurisdiction shall apply to such trust as of the date specified in such designation. Any such designation shall be in writing.

IN WITNESS WHEREOF, the Grantors and the Trustee have hereunto set their hands as of the date first above written.

_____, Grantor

_____, Grantor

_____, Trustee

THE STATE OF TEXAS §
§
COUNTY OF _____ §

Before me, the undersigned authority, on this day personally appeared _____, who produced a driver's license issued by the State of Texas that contained his photograph and signature as identification thereby proving him to be the person whose name is subscribed to the foregoing instrument as Grantor, and acknowledged to me that he executed the same for the purposes and consideration therein expressed.

Given under my hand and seal of office, on _____, 2009.

Notary Public, State of Texas

THE STATE OF TEXAS §
§
COUNTY OF _____ §

Before me, the undersigned authority, on this day personally appeared _____, who produced a driver's license issued by the State of Texas that contained her photograph and signature as identification thereby proving her to be the person whose name is subscribed to the foregoing instrument as Grantor, and acknowledged to me that she executed the same for the purposes and consideration therein expressed.

Given under my hand and seal of office, on _____, 2009.

Notary Public, State of Texas

THE STATE OF TEXAS §
§
COUNTY OF _____ §

Before me, the undersigned authority, on this day personally appeared _____, who produced a driver's license issued by the State of Texas that contained his photograph and signature as identification thereby proving him to be the person whose name is subscribed to the foregoing instrument as Trustee, and acknowledged to me that he executed the same for the purposes and consideration therein expressed and in the capacity therein stated.

Given under my hand and seal of office, on _____, 2009.

Notary Public, State of Texas

3) Powers of attorney (form 3)

I would suggest a clause:

In the event that I have disappeared in a Rapture like disappearance, I direct that those persons whom I have designated with the power of attorney to be able to continue to use this power of attorney until such time as my last Will and Testament has been admitted to probate, at which time the powers and authority granted hereunder shall cease and cancel.

Then follow with your normal power of attorney
(Valid in Texas:)

STATUTORY DURABLE POWER OF ATTORNEY

NOTICE: THE POWERS GRANTED BY THIS DOCUMENT ARE BROAD AND SWEEPING. THEY ARE EXPLAINED IN THE DURABLE POWER OF ATTORNEY ACT, CHAPTER XII, TEXAS PROBATE CODE. IF YOU HAVE ANY QUESTIONS

ABOUT THESE POWERS, OBTAIN COMPETENT LEGAL ADVICE. THIS DOCUMENT DOES NOT AUTHORIZE ANYONE TO MAKE MEDICAL AND OTHER HEALTH-CARE DECISIONS FOR YOU. YOU MAY REVOKE THIS POWER OF ATTORNEY IF YOU LATER WISH TO DO SO.

I, _____, with an address of _____, _____, Texas _____, appoint my father, ____ _____, with an address of _____, _____ _____, _____ _____, as my agent to act for me in any lawful way with respect to all of the following powers except for a power that I have crossed out below. If ____ _____ dies, becomes legally disabled, resigns, or ceases to act, I appoint my father, _____, with an address of _____, _____, _____ _____, as my agent. If _____ dies, becomes legally disabled, resigns, or ceases to act, I appoint, as my agent.

TO WITHHOLD A POWER, YOU MUST CROSS OUT EACH POWER WITHHELD.

Real property transactions;

Tangible personal property transactions;

Stock and bond transactions;

Commodity and option transactions;

Banking and other financial institution transactions;

Business operating transactions;

Insurance and annuity transactions;

Estate, trust and other beneficiary transactions;

Claims and litigation;

Personal and family maintenance;

Benefits from social security, Medicare, Medicaid, or other governmental programs or civil or military service;

Retirement plan transactions;

Tax matters.

IF NO POWER LISTED ABOVE IS CROSSED OUT, THIS DOCUMENT SHALL BE CONSTRUED AND INTERPRETED AS A GENERAL POWER OF ATTORNEY, AND MY AGENT (ATTORNEY IN FACT) SHALL HAVE THE POWER AND AUTHORITY TO PERFORM OR UNDERTAKE ANY ACTION I COULD PERFORM OR UNDERTAKE IF I WERE PERSONALLY PRESENT.

SPECIAL INSTRUCTIONS

GIFTS: Special instructions applicable to gifts (initial in front of the following sentence to have it apply):

_____ I grant my agent the power to apply my property to make gifts, and specifically, my agent may make gifts of my property as enumerated in Sections (1) and (2) below under the heading ADDITIONAL POWERS.

LIMITATIONS: Notwithstanding any provision herein to the contrary, any authority granted to my agent shall be limited so as to prevent this power of attorney from causing my agent to be taxed on my income (unless my agent is my spouse) and from causing my assets to be subject to a general power of appointment by my agent, as that term is defined in Section 2041 of the Internal Revenue Code of 1986, as amended (the "Code").

MULTIPLE AGENTS: When multiple agents are serving jointly under this power of attorney, then all of them must act or sign together. Furthermore, when multiple agents are named or serving hereunder and any one or more, but not all, die, become legally disabled, resign, or refuse to act, then the remaining agent or agents, as the case may be, shall be appointed or continue to serve in such capacity.

ADDITIONAL POWERS: ON THE FOLLOWING LINES YOU MAY GIVE SPECIAL INSTRUCTIONS LIMITING OR EXTENDING THE POWERS GRANTED TO YOUR AGENT.

In addition to the powers granted above, I grant to my agent all of the following powers:

(1) If I have initialed the line above granting my agent the power to apply my property to make gifts, then in addition to such power, I further grant to my agent the power to make gifts of any of my property to or to pay amounts on behalf of (including transfers which are made outright, in trust or otherwise) any one or more of my descendants (including my agent, if my agent is a descendant of mine) or to any charitable organization to which deductible gifts may be made under the income and gift tax provisions of the Code. Such gifts or amounts paid to my descendants shall include those which are excludible under Section 2503(b)

or Section 2503(e) of the Code or those to which the split gift provisions of Section 2513 of the Code are expected to apply. Nothing herein shall be construed to require any court action whatsoever prior to making such gifts, nor to restrict such gifts to a situation in which it must be determined that I will remain incapacitated for the remainder of my lifetime. Notwithstanding the foregoing, the gifts made by a person who is serving as my agent under this instrument to himself or herself shall not exceed in the aggregate for any calendar year the greater of five thousand dollars ($5,000) or five percent (5%) of the fair market value of my estate (for U.S. gift tax purposes) as of December 31st of such calendar year; provided, however, if my agent is making gifts authorized by the following paragraph of this power of attorney in order to obtain or maintain eligibility for public health care benefits, then these limitations shall not apply.

(2) If I have initialed the line above granting my agent the power to apply my property to make gifts, and if my agent in my agent's sole discretion has determined that I need nursing home or other long-term medical care and that I will receive proper medical care whether I privately pay for such care or

if I am a recipient of Title XIX (Medicaid) or other public benefits, then my agent shall have the power: (i) to take any and all steps necessary, in my agent's judgment, to obtain and maintain my eligibility for any and all public benefits and entitlement programs, including, if necessary, creating and funding a qualified income trust or special needs trust for me, my wife or a disabled child, if any; (ii) to transfer with or without consideration my assets to my wife and/or my descendants (if any), or to my natural heirs at law or to the persons named as beneficiaries under my last will and testament or a revocable living trust which I or my agent may have established, including my agent; and (iii) to enter into a personal services contract for my benefit, including entering into such contract with my agent, and even if doing so may be considered self-dealing. Such public benefits and entitlement programs shall include, but are not limited to, Social Security, Supplemental Security Income, Medicare, Medicaid and Veterans benefits.

(3) The power to take legal action to compel third parties to recognize the validity of this instrument, and the power to

sue for damages, both punitive and actual, in the case of a refusal by a third party to honor this power.

(4)　The power to create for me (and with my wife as to any property owned by my wife or in which my wife has any interest which may be transferred) one or more revocable trusts (referred to as a "grantor trust") of which I am an income beneficiary and with such person or persons as my agent shall select as the trustee or co-trustees (including my agent or any corporate trustee having capital and surplus at the time of its appointment in excess of $10,000,000.00), without bond or other security, and with such other terms and provisions as my agent shall deem appropriate, including, but not limited to, provisions to minimize or eliminate any death or transfer taxes which may be imposed on my estate, any grantor trust, any beneficiary of my estate or any beneficiary of any grantor trust, and to grant to the trustee or co-trustees of any grantor trust any one or more of the powers granted to a trustee under the Texas Trust Code, as amended; provided, however, such trust agreement shall provide that I retain the power to revoke any such grantor trust, in whole or in part at any time, or that I have a general power of appointment over the assets of such grantor trust; and further provided that at my death the assets of any such grantor trust which would have constituted my community property if such assets had not been transferred to such grantor trust, together with all of such assets which would have constituted any separate property if such assets had not been transferred to such grantor trust, shall pass in a manner which is consistent with any existing estate plan which I may have previously instituted, including dispositions of my property by will, trust, beneficiary designation, or otherwise, and including the apportionment of taxes and other expenses, or if there is no person named in such grantor trust to whom such assets shall pass, then such assets shall be delivered to the personal representative of my estate. It is not my intention in granting the power enumerated in this paragraph to allow my agent to change in any way the persons who will be receiving the property of my estate or the overall scheme of my estate plan; rather, I am attempting to facilitate my agent's ability to save taxes or otherwise reduce the costs of administering my estate. If I have already established a grantor trust, or if my agent creates a grantor trust for me, this paragraph shall include the power to alter, amend or modify such grantor trust in a manner which is consistent with the provisions contained herein; and in addition, any such grantor trust created by me or by my agent may be revoked by my agent as long as such revocation results in a disposition of my estate which is consistent with my existing estate plan. Further, my agent shall have the power to transfer all or part of the interest I may own in any real property, stocks, bonds, accounts with financial institutions, insurance, and other property to the trustee of such grantor trust.

(5) The power to exercise my rights to manage the community estate of my wife and myself if I am married at such time (which power shall be presumptively exercised to its fullest extent unless otherwise provided), and the power to enter into partition or other marital agreements between my wife and me.

(6) The power to make, execute and deliver oil, gas and mineral leases upon all lands and mineral interests owned or claimed by me, wheresoever located, to such persons and upon such terms and conditions as my agent may deem advisable. Such oil, gas and mineral leases may be for such duration

and contain such warranties of title, pooling and unitization provisions, and other special clauses as my agent may agree to upon my behalf. This power shall include the right to negotiate and contract for the sale of any such oil, gas and mineral lease or leases. I also give my agent the power and authority to execute pooling or unitization agreements affecting any oil, gas or other mineral rights or interests owned or claimed by me, whether mineral fee interests, royalty interests or leasehold interests, so as to pool and combine any such interest or interests with the interests of others in the same or other lands, such agreements to be upon such terms and conditions and to contain such authorizations as my agent may deem advisable.

(7) The power to appoint or substitute one or more agents to serve as my agent under this power of attorney; provided, however, such power shall be exercisable only by the then-serving agent (or if more than one agent is serving, by all such agents acting unanimously), and any such appointment or substitution shall override other provisions contained herein which may attempt to name one or more successor agents. Any such appointment or substitution may be revoked by

me or my agent at any time and for any reason, and such appointment or substitution shall not terminate upon the death, disability, incapacity or resignation of my agent. Any such appointment or substitution shall be evidenced by acknowledged written instrument.

(8) The power to pay a reasonable fee from my estate to my agent as compensation for services rendered under this power of attorney in an amount which does not exceed the customary and prevailing charges for services of a similar character at the time and place such services are performed.

(9) The power to represent me, and to appoint an agent or agents to represent me, before the Internal Revenue Service or any State or other taxing authority by completing, signing, and submitting IRS Form 2848 or any other governmental form.

(10) In addition to the powers enumerated above, I hereby give and grant unto my said agent full power and authority to do and perform all and every act and thing whatsoever requisite and necessary to be done, as fully, to all intents and purposes, as I might or could do if personally present, hereby ratifying

and confirming whatsoever my said agent shall and may do by virtue hereof; provided, however, and notwithstanding the foregoing, if I have deleted a particular power or several powers on page one of this power of attorney, then my agent shall not have such power or powers by virtue of the power and authority conferred by this sentence.

This power of attorney becomes effective upon my disability or incapacity. I shall be considered disabled or incapacitated for purposes of this power of attorney if a physician certifies in writing at a date later than the date this power of attorney is executed that, based on the physician's medical examination of me, I am mentally incapable of managing my financial affairs. I authorize the physician who examines me for this purpose to disclose my physical or mental condition to another person for purposes of this power of attorney. A third party who accepts this power of attorney is fully protected from any action taken under this power of attorney that is based on the determination made by a physician of my disability or incapacity.

I agree that any third party who receives a copy of this document may act under it. Revocation of the durable power of attorney is not effective as to a third party until the third party receives actual notice of the revocation. I agree to indemnify the third party for any claims that arise against the third party because of reliance on this power of attorney.

I agree that any third party dealing with any alternate agent or agents named hereunder may rely on a written and acknowledged affidavit signed by such alternate agent or agents stating that all prior agents have died, become legally disabled, resigned or refused to serve, and no third party shall be required to investigate as to whether such affidavit is correct. Such affidavit need not state specific details regarding the reasons why the prior agents are not able to serve, but instead, such affidavit may simply state that such death, disability, resignation or refusal to act has occurred. I agree to indemnify the third party for any claims that arise against the third party because of reliance on such affidavit.

Signed on _____, 2009.

_____, Principal

THE STATE OF TEXAS §
§
COUNTY OF _____ §

Before me, the undersigned authority, on this day personally appeared _____, who produced a driver's license issued by the State of Texas that contained his photograph and signature as identification thereby proving him to be the person whose name is subscribed to the foregoing instrument as Principal, and acknowledged to me that he executed the same for the purposes and consideration therein expressed.

Given under my hand and seal of office, on _____, 2009.

Notary Public, State of Texas

THE ATTORNEY IN FACT OR AGENT, BY ACCEPTING OR ACTING UNDER THE APPOINTMENT, ASSUMES THE FIDUCIARY AND OTHER LEGAL RESPONSIBILITIES OF AN AGENT.

Instructions (Form four) see chapter four

"INSTRUCTIONS TO MY LOVED ONES:

These instructions are to be used in the event of my death or my disappearance in what is commonly referred to as "the rapture of the church". I do not intend this to be my Will, nor and attempt to modify my Will. These are merely instruction to assist those I leave behind."

Then follow with instructions which would help those you left behind to understand the location and make up of assets and liabilities and advice regarding people from whom to seek advice, who you need to be careful of in dealings, etc.

Form five: health care power of attorney FOR USE IN Texas only (Chapter 8)

COMBINATION DIRECTIVE TO PHYSICIANS AND FAMILY OR SURROGATES AND MEDICAL POWER OF ATTORNEY

PART I: DIRECTIVE TO PHYSICIANS

I, _____, recognize that the best health care is based upon a partnership of trust and communication with my physician. My physician and I will make health care decisions together as long as I am of sound mind and able to make my wishes known. If there comes a time that I am unable to make medical decisions about myself because of illness or injury, I direct that the following treatment preferences be honored:

Terminal Condition. If, in the judgment of my physician, I am suffering with a terminal condition from which I am expected to die within six months, even with available life-sustaining treatment provided in accordance with prevailing standards of medical care:

A. _____ I request that all treatments other than those needed to keep me comfortable be discontinued or withheld and my physician allow me to die as gently as possible; OR

B. _____ I request that I be kept alive in this terminal condition using available life-sustaining treatment. (THIS SELECTION DOES NOT APPLY TO HOSPICE CARE.)

Irreversible Condition. If, in the judgment of my physician, I am suffering with an irreversible condition so that I cannot care for myself or make decisions for myself and am expected to die without life-sustaining treatment provided in accordance with prevailing standards of care:

C. _____ I request that all treatments other than those needed to keep me comfortable be discontinued or withheld and my physician allow me to die as gently as possible; OR

D. _____ I request that I be kept alive in this irreversible condition using available life-sustaining treatment. (THIS SELECTION DOES NOT APPLY TO HOSPICE CARE.)

After signing this document, if my representative or I elect hospice care, I understand and agree that only those treatments needed to keep me comfortable would be provided, and I would not be given available life-sustaining treatments.

If, in the judgment of my physician, my death is imminent within minutes to hours, even with the use of all available medical treatment provided within the prevailing standard of care, I acknowledge that all treatments may be withheld or removed except those needed to maintain my comfort. This directive will remain in effect until I revoke it. No other person may do so.

Additional Requests. (After discussion with your physician, you may wish to consider listing particular treatments in this space that you do or do not want in specific circumstances, such as artificial nutrition and fluids, intravenous antibiotics, etc. Be sure to state whether you do or do not want the particular treatment.)

_____

_____

_____

_____

Instructions For Completing This Document. This is an important legal document. It is designed to help you communicate your wishes about medical treatment at some time in the future when you are unable to make your wishes known because of illness or injury. These wishes are usually based on personal values. In particular, you may want to consider what burdens or hardships of treatment you would be willing to accept for a particular amount of benefit obtained if you were seriously ill. You are encouraged to discuss your values and wishes with your family or chosen spokesperson, as well as your physician. Your physician, other health care provider, or medical institution may provide you with various resources to assist you in completing this document. Brief definitions are listed below and may aid you in your discussions and advance planning. Initial the treatment choices that best reflect your personal preferences. Provide a copy of this document to your physician, usual hospital, and family or spokesperson. Consider a periodic review of this document. By periodic review, you can best assure that the directive reflects your preferences. In addition to this document, Texas law provides for another type of directive that can be important during a serious illness called an Out-of-Hospital Do-Not-Resuscitate Order. You may wish to discuss this document with your physician, family, hospital representative, or other advisers. You may also wish to complete a directive related to the donation of organs and tissues.

PART II. MEDICAL POWER OF ATTORNEY

I, _____, appoint:

Name:
Address:
Phone:

as my agent to make any and all health care decisions for me. This designation takes effect if I become unable to make my own health care decisions and this fact is certified in writing by my physician.

DESIGNATION OF ALTERNATE AGENT

If the person designated as my agent is unable or unwilling to make health care decisions for me, I designate the following person as my agent to make health care decisions for me as authorized by this document:

Name:
Address: _____-
_____

Phone: _____

IN THE EVENT BOTH SUCH INDIVIDUALS HAVE BEEN TAKEN IN WHAT COULD ONLY BE DESCRIBED AS THE RAPTURE OF THE CHURCH, I REQUEST MY _____ _____ TO ACT IN THEIR PLACE AND STEAD.

LIMITATIONS

Limitations on the decision-making authority of my agent are as follows:

If I am a beneficiary under a life or accident insurance policy, on a right of survivorship agreement, under a will or trust agreement, or under any other arrangement, and my agent has personal knowledge of this fact, and if the withholding or withdrawal of life-sustaining treatment would shorten the period of my survival such that I, my family, my beneficiaries or my heirs would suffer the loss of a bequest, inheritance or other nonprobate asset, then my agent is authorized in my agent's full discretion to consider this factor when refusing or withdrawing life-sustaining treatment, as long as my agent's decision does not cause me further suffering.

ORIGINAL

The original of this document is kept at:

COPIES

DURATION

I understand that my designation of a health care agent will exist indefinitely from the date I execute this document unless I establish a shorter time or revoke such designation. However, if I do establish a shorter time for such designation and if I am unable to make health care decisions for myself when such time period does expire, the authority I have granted my agent shall, nevertheless, continue to exist until the time I become able to make health care decisions for myself.

PRIOR DESIGNATIONS REVOKED

I revoke any prior durable power of attorney for health care and any prior medical power of attorney.

ACKNOWLEDGMENT OF DISCLOSURE STATEMENT

I have been provided with a disclosure statement explaining the effect of this document. I have read and understand the information contained in the disclosure statement.

City, County, and State of Residence: _____, _____

_____ County, Texas

Signed on _____, 200___.

_____

Declarant and Principal

STATEMENTS OF WITNESSES

Two competent adult witnesses must sign below, acknowledging the signature of the declarant.

STATEMENT OF FIRST WITNESS.

I am not the person appointed as agent by this document. I am not related to the principal by blood or marriage. I would not be entitled to any portion of the principal's estate on the principal's death. I am not the attending physician of the principal or an employee of the attending physician. I have no claim against any portion of the principal's estate on the principal's death. Furthermore, if I am an employee of a health care facility in which the principal is a patient, I am not involved in providing direct patient care to the principal and am not an officer, director, partner, or business office employee of the health care facility or of any parent organization of the health care facility.

Witness Signature:
Print Name:
Address:
Date: , 200___

STATEMENT OF SECOND WITNESS.

I am not the person appointed as agent by this document. I am not related to the principal by blood or marriage. I would not be entitled to any portion of the principal's estate on the principal's death. I am not the attending physician of the principal or an employee of the attending physician. I have no claim against any portion of the principal's estate on the principal's death. Furthermore, if I am an employee of a health care facility in which the principal is a patient, I am not involved in providing direct patient care to the principal and am not an officer, director, partner, or business office employee of the health care facility or of any parent organization of the health care facility.

Witness Signature:
Print Name:
Address:
Date: , 200___

THE STATE OF TEXAS   §
              §
COUNTY OF _____   §

BEFORE ME, the undersigned authority, on this day personally appeared _____, known to me to be the person whose name is subscribed to the foregoing instrument as Declarant and Principal, and who, having been duly sworn, states that such Declarant/Principal executed this Combination Directive to Physicians and Family or Surrogates and Medical Power of Attorney in the presence of two witnesses and for the purposes and consideration therein expressed.

GIVEN UNDER MY HAND AND SEAL OF OFFICE, on ___ _____, 200_____.

NOTARY PUBLIC IN AND FOR
THE STATE OF TEXAS

Notary's printed name:

My commission expires:

THIS IS AN IMPORTANT LEGAL DOCUMENT REGARDING YOUR MEDICAL POWER OF ATTORNEY. BEFORE SIGNING

THIS DOCUMENT, YOU SHOULD KNOW THESE IMPORTANT FACTS:

Except to the extent you state otherwise, this document gives the person you name as your agent the authority to make any and all health care decisions for you in accordance with your wishes, including your religious and moral beliefs, when you are no longer capable of making them yourself. Because "health care" means any treatment, service or procedure to maintain, diagnose, or treat your physical or mental condition, your agent has the power to make a broad range of health care decisions for you. Your agent may consent, refuse to consent or withdraw consent to medical treatment and may make decisions about withdrawing or withholding life-sustaining treatment. Your agent may not consent to voluntary inpatient mental health services, convulsive treatment, psychosurgery or abortion. A physician must comply with your agent's instructions or allow you to be transferred to another physician. Your agent's authority begins when your doctor certifies that you lack the competence to make health care decisions. Your agent is obligated to follow your instructions when making decisions on your behalf. Unless you state otherwise, your agent has the same authority to make decisions about your health care as you would have had.

The Rapture, How Will You Prepare For It?

It is important that you discuss this document with your physician or other health care provider before you sign it to make sure that you understand the nature and range of decisions that may be made on your behalf. If you do not have a physician, you should talk with someone else who is knowledgeable about these issues and can answer your questions. You do not need a lawyer's assistance to complete this document, but if there is anything in this document that you do not understand, you should ask a lawyer to explain it to you. The person you appoint as agent should be someone you know and trust. The person must be 18 years of age or older or a person under 18 years of age who has had the disabilities of minority removed. If you appoint your health or residential care provider (e.g., your physician or an employee of a home health agency, hospital, nursing home or residential care home, other than a relative), that person has to choose between acting as your agent or as your health or residential care provider; the law does not permit a person to do both at the same time.

You should inform the person you appoint that you want the person to be your health care agent. You should discuss this document with your agent and your physician and give each a signed copy. You should indicate on the document itself the people and institutions who have copies of the signed originals. Your agent is not liable for health care decisions made in good faith on your behalf. Even after you have signed this document, you have the right to make health care decisions for yourself as long as you are able to do so and treatment cannot be given to you or stopped over your objection. You have the right to revoke the authority granted to your agent by informing your agent or your health or residential care provider orally or in writing, or by your execution of a subsequent medical power of attorney. This document may not be changed or modified. If you want to make changes in the document, you must make an entirely new one. You may wish to designate an alternate agent in the event that your agent is unwilling, unable or ineligible to act as your agent. Any alternate agent you designate has the same authority to make health care decisions for you.

THIS POWER OF ATTORNEY IS NOT VALID UNLESS IT IS SIGNED IN THE PRESENCE OF TWO COMPETENT ADULT WITNESSES. THE FOLLOWING PERSONS MAY NOT ACT AS ONE OF THE WITNESSES:

(1) the person you have designated as your agent;

(2) a person related to you by blood or marriage;

(3) a person entitled to any part of your estate after your death under a will or codicil executed by you or by operation of law;

(4) your attending physician;

(5) an employee of your attending physician;

(6) an employee of a health care facility in which you are a patient if the employee is providing direct patient care to you or is an officer, director, partner, or business office employee of the health care facility or of any parent organization of the health care facility; or

(7) a person who, at the time this power of attorney is executed, has a claim against any part of your estate after your death.

I have read and understand the contents of this disclosure statement.

Date: _____, 200_____.

_____

Definitions:

"Artificial nutrition and hydration" means the provision of nutrients or fluids by a tube inserted in a vein, under the skin in the subcutaneous tissues, or in the stomach (gastrointestinal tract).

"Irreversible condition" means a condition, injury, or illness:

    (1)   that may be treated, but is never cured or eliminated;

    (2)   that leaves a person unable to care for or make decisions for the person's own self; and

    (3)   that, without life-sustaining treatment provided in accordance with the prevailing standard of medical care, is fatal.

Explanation: Many serious illnesses such as cancer, failure of major organs (kidney, heart, liver, or lung), and serious brain disease such as Alzheimer's dementia may be considered irreversible early on. There is no cure, but the patient may be kept alive for prolonged periods of time if the patient receives life-sustaining treatments. Late in the course of the same illness, the disease may be considered terminal when, even with treatment, the patient is expected to die. You may wish to consider which burdens of treatment you would be willing to accept in an effort to achieve a particular outcome. This is a very personal decision that you may wish to discuss with your physician, family, or other important persons in your life.

"Life-sustaining treatment" means treatment that, based on reasonable medical judgment, sustains the life of a patient and without which the patient will die. The term includes both life-sustaining medications and artificial life support such as mechanical breathing machines, kidney dialysis treatment, and artificial hydration and nutrition. The term does not include the administration of pain management medication, the performance of a medical procedure necessary to provide comfort care, or any other medical care provided to alleviate a patient's pain.

"Terminal condition" means an incurable condition caused by injury, disease, or illness that according to reasonable medical judgment will produce death within six months, even with available life-sustaining treatment provided in accordance with the prevailing standard of medical care.

Explanation: Many serious illnesses may be considered irreversible early in the course of the illness, but they may not be considered terminal until the disease is fairly advanced. In thinking about terminal illness and its treatment, you again may wish to consider the relative benefits and burdens of treatment and discuss your wishes with your physician, family, or other important persons in your life.

End of Texas health care power of attorney

Chapter thirty six

Bibliography

The Ryrie Study Bible, New American Standard Translation

Rev. 3: 10-13; 6:15- 17; 20: 4-15;

Matt 24:21-44

1 Thess 4: 16-18; 5:1-11

2 Thess 2: 1-17

Daniel 9:27

1 Corinthians 15:51-58

Chapter 37

c.v.

THOMAS G. BOUSQUET

9225 Katy Freeway, Suite 103

Houston, Texas 77024

tgb@bousquetdevine.com

Thomas G. Bousquet is 75 years old and is a lifelong resident of Houston, Texas. He continues practicing law in Houston where he has practiced law in excess of 51 years and in Brenham where he has opened a law and real estate office. He is a graduate of the University of Texas (B.A., 1956) and the University of Texas Law School (J.D., 1958). He has been licensed to practice law in Texas since April 24, 1958. He has been AV rated (highest rating) by Martindale-Hubbell Law Directory since 1969. He has been both Secretary and Vice President of the Houston Bar Association and

Special Assistant Disciplinary Counsel to the Texas Commission for Lawyer Discipline. He was certified by the Texas Board of Legal Specialization in Civil Trial Law between 1979 and 2003 and in Family Law between 1975 and 2003. He was a member of the American Academy of Matrimonial Lawyers for twenty years. He is past President of the Texas Association of Certified Civil Trial Lawyers. He is a founding member and secretary of the National Academy of Legal Malpractice Attorneys. His practice over 51 years has included extensive civil trial, real estate, corporate and estate planning experience. He is admitted to practice before the U.S. District Court for the Southern District of Texas, the Fifth Circuit and the U.S. Supreme Court (1971). He has been a lecturer at several State Bar Association institutes and seminars at both the South Texas Law School and the Tulane University School of Law. He has had articles published in the Texas State Bar Journal, the magazine of the Family Law Section of the State Bar of Texas and in the National Law Office Economics and Management Journal. He has been quoted as an expert in Legal Malpractice in The National Law Journal, Texas Lawyer, Lawyer's Weekly, The New York Times and The Boston Globe. He is a member of the Christian Legal Society and is a Life Fellow of the Texas Bar Foundation.

CPSIA information can be obtained
at www.ICGtesting.com
Printed in the USA
BVHW071257130920
588715BV00004B/411